The Psalms Project Volume Eleven

Discovering the Spiritual World through the Psalms – Psalm 101 - 110

Michael Harvey Koplitz

TABLE OF CONTENTS

The goal of this project:

This research project will examine the 150 psalms for the spiritual awareness each Psalm offers. Each Psalm will be examined by its language and the commentary of the Sages. The spiritual awareness analysis will be done in alignment with Ari's definition of the Tree of life, the Book of Creation, and the Zohar. Each verse of the Psalm will be rewritten using the intent of the language and spiritual commentary to convey its spiritual lesson.

The main resources:

> The Zohar
>
> The Book of Creation
>
> Ari's writing on the Tree of Life and the Ten Sefirot
>
> The Theological Wordbook of the Old Testament
>
> Samson Hirsch's commentary on the Psalms
>
> Tehillim – Psalms – A new translation with a commentary anthologized from the Talmudic and rabbinic sources
>
> Accordance Bible Software

Psalm 101

New American Standard 1995	Hebrew
Psa. 101:0 A Psalm of David. **Psa. 101:1** I will *sing of lovingkindness and [1]justice, 　To You, O LORD, I will sing praises. 2　I will [1a]give heed to the [2]blameless way. 　When will You come to me? 　I will walk within my house in the [3b]integrity of my heart. 3　I will set no *worthless thing before my eyes; 　I hate the [1]work of those who *fall away; 　It shall not fasten its grip on me. 4　A *perverse heart shall depart from me; 　I will know no evil. 5　Whoever secretly *slanders his neighbor, him I will [1]destroy; 　No one who has a *haughty look and an arrogant heart will I endure. **Psa. 101:6** My eyes shall be upon the faithful of the land, that they may dwell with me; 　He who walks in a [1a]blameless way is the one who will minister to me. 7　He who *practices deceit shall not dwell within my house; 　He who speaks falsehood *shall not [1]maintain his position before me. 8　*Every morning I will [1b]destroy all the wicked of the land,	‎**Psa. 101:1** לְדָוִד מִזְמוֹר חֶסֶד־ וּמִשְׁפָּט אָשִׁירָה לְךָ יְהוָה אֲזַמֵּרָה׃ ² אַשְׂכִּילָה ׀ בְּדֶרֶךְ תָּמִים מָתַי תָּבוֹא אֵלָי אֶתְהַלֵּךְ בְּתָם־לְבָבִי בְּקֶרֶב בֵּיתִי׃ ³ לֹא־אָשִׁית ׀ לְנֶגֶד עֵינַי דְּבַר־בְּלִיָּעַל עֲשֹׂה־סֵטִים שָׂנֵאתִי לֹא יִדְבַּק בִּי׃ ⁴ לֵבָב עִקֵּשׁ יָסוּר מִמֶּנִּי רָע לֹא אֵדָע׃ ⁵ מְלֹשְׁנִי [מְלָשְׁנִי] בַסֵּתֶר ׀ רֵעֵהוּ אוֹתוֹ אַצְמִית גְּבַהּ־עֵינַיִם וּרְחַב לֵבָב אֹתוֹ לֹא אוּכָל׃ ⁶ עֵינַי ׀ בְּנֶאֶמְנֵי־ אֶרֶץ לָשֶׁבֶת עִמָּדִי הֹלֵךְ בְּדֶרֶךְ תָּמִים הוּא יְשָׁרְתֵנִי׃ ⁷ לֹא־יֵשֵׁב ׀ בְּקֶרֶב בֵּיתִי עֹשֵׂה רְמִיָּה דֹּבֵר שְׁקָרִים לֹא־יִכּוֹן לְנֶגֶד עֵינָי׃ ⁸ לַבְּקָרִים אַצְמִית כָּל־רִשְׁעֵי־אָרֶץ לְהַכְרִית מֵעִיר־יְהוָה כָּל־פֹּעֲלֵי אָוֶן׃

<table>
<tr><td>So as to [c]cut off from the [d]city of the LORD all those who do iniquity.</td><td></td></tr>
</table>

References

Psalm 101:1
[1]Or *judgment*
[a]Ps 51:14; 89:1; 145:7

Psalm 101:2
[1]Or *behave prudently in*
[2]Or *way of integrity*
[3]Or *blamelessness*
[a]1 Sam 18:5, 14
[b]1 Kin 9:4

Psalm 101:3
[1]Or *practice of apostasy*
[a]Deut 15:9
[b]Josh 23:6; Ps 40:4

Psalm 101:4
[a]Prov 11:20

Psalm 101:5
[1]Or *silence*
[a]Ps 50:20; Jer 9:4
[b]Ps 10:4; 18:27; Prov 6:17

Psalm 101:6
[1]Or *way of integrity*
[a]Ps 119:1

Psalm 101:7
[1]Lit *be established before my eyes*
[a]Ps 43:1; 52:2
[b]Ps 52:4, 5

Psalm 101:8
[1]Or *silence*
[a]Jer 21:12
[b]Ps 75:10
[c]Ps 118:10-12

[d]Ps 46:4; 48:2, 8

Targum

Psa. 101:1 Composed by David, a psalm. Whether you show mercy to me or treat me with justice, for both of them I will sing praise; in your presence, O LORD, I will make music. **2** God said, "I will make you wise in the perfect way; when will you come unto me?" David said, "I will walk in the perfection of my heart within my house of instruction." **3** I will not set upon my heart the word of the wicked man, the ones who do evil; and those who wander from the commandments I hate, they will not follow me. **4** Let the twisted heart pass from me; I shall not know the evil impulse. **5** He who relates slander against his fellow – him will I overturn; and he who walks with haughty eyes will be stricken with leprosy; with him I will never dwell. **6** My eyes are on the honest of the land, to dwell in the precincts of the righteous; he who walks perfect on the way – he shall stand among my ministers. **7** He who acts guilefully will not dwell in the midst of my sanctuary; he who speaks lies has no right to stand before my eyes. **8** In the age to come, which is likened to the light of morning, I will overturn all the wicked of the earth, to destroy from Jerusalem, the city of the LORD, all those who work deceit.

Spiritual Awareness

Introduction

King David contemplated the wonders of the LORD through nature. One of the miracles of the LORD is the birth of a baby. This Psalm is a song of inspiration that came to David. It describes how David secluded himself. He hated evil and had a sincere love for strict justice.

Verse one

David calls out to the Sefirah Chesed for the LORD's love.

I will sing to the Sefirah Chesed for the LORD's love, and to the Sefirah Gevurah for justice, LORD, I address my song.

Notes of the Psalm

The Scriptures are not afraid to tell stories about the fall of heroes. King David was the most beloved of the Kings of Israel. However, he did commit a couple of sins that the LORD forgave him. Yes, David had flaws, and the Scriptures want us to know that even the best person can fail. David was punished for this act of adultery and murder by the death of the baby that was conceived with Bathsheba. After his repentance, the next child of Bathsheba was Solomon, who followed David as king and built the LORD's Temple. David was told by the LORD that he could not produce the Temple. Instead, David gathered the building materials needed for the project. David wanted the LORD's love and justice to help him rule over the land.

Psalm 102

New American Standard 1995	Hebrew
Psa. 102:0 A Prayer of the Afflicted when he is faint and †pours out his complaint before the LORD. **Psa. 102:1** ᵃHear my prayer, O LORD! And let my cry for help ᵇcome to You. 2 ᵃDo not hide Your face from me in the day of my distress; ᵇIncline Your ear to me; In the day when I call ᵃanswer me quickly. 3 For my days ᵃhave been ¹consumed in smoke, And my ᵇbones have been scorched like a hearth. 4 My heart ᵃhas been smitten like ¹grass and has ᵇwithered away, Indeed, I ᶜforget to eat my bread. 5 Because of the ¹loudness of my groaning My ᵃbones ²cling to my flesh. 6 I ¹resemble a ᵃpelican of the wilderness; I have become like an owl of the waste places. 7 I ᵃlie awake, I have become like a lonely bird on a housetop. **Psa. 102:8** My enemies ᵃhave reproached me all day long; Those who ¹ᵇderide me ²have used my *name* as a ᶜcurse. 9 For I have eaten ashes like bread	תְּפִלָּה לְעָנִי כִי־יַעֲטֹף **Psa. 102:1** וְלִפְנֵי יְהֹוָה יִשְׁפֹּךְ שִׂיחֹו ׃ ² יְהֹוָה שִׁמְעָה תְפִלָּתִי וְשַׁוְעָתִי אֵלֶיךָ תָבֹוא ׃ ³ אַל־תַּסְתֵּר פָּנֶיךָ ׀ מִמֶּנִּי בְּיֹום צַר לִי הַטֵּה־אֵלַי אָזְנֶךָ בְּיֹום אֶקְרָא מַהֵר עֲנֵנִי ׃ ⁴ כִּי־כָלוּ בְעָשָׁן יָמָי וְעַצְמֹותַי כְּמֹו־קֵד נִחָרוּ ׃ ⁵ הוּכָּה־כָעֵשֶׂב וַיִּבַשׁ לִבִּי כִּי־ שָׁכַחְתִּי מֵאֲכֹל לַחְמִי ׃ ⁶ מִקֹּול אַנְחָתִי דָּבְקָה עַצְמִי לִבְשָׂרִי ׃ ⁷ דָּמִיתִי לִקְאַת מִדְבָּר הָיִיתִי כְּכֹוס חֳרָבֹות ׃ ⁸ שָׁקַדְתִּי וָאֶהְיֶה כְּצִפֹּור בֹּודֵד עַל־גָּג ׃ ⁹ כָּל־הַיֹּום חֵרְפוּנִי אֹויְבָי מְהֹולָלַי בִּי נִשְׁבָּעוּ ׃ ¹⁰ כִּי־ אֵפֶר כַּלֶּחֶם אָכָלְתִּי וְשִׁקֻּוַי בִּבְכִי מָסָכְתִּי ׃ ¹¹ מִפְּנֵי־זַעַמְךָ וְקִצְפֶּךָ כִּי נְשָׂאתַנִי וַתַּשְׁלִיכֵנִי ׃ ¹² יָמַי כְּצֵל נָטוּי וַאֲנִי כָּעֵשֶׂב אִיבָשׁ ׃ ¹³ וְאַתָּה יְהֹוָה לְעֹולָם תֵּשֵׁב וְזִכְרְךָ לְדֹר וָדֹר ׃ ¹⁴ אַתָּה תָקוּם תְּרַחֵם צִיֹּון כִּי־ עֵת לְחֶנְנָהּ כִּי־בָא מֹועֵד ׃ ¹⁵ כִּי־ רָצוּ עֲבָדֶיךָ אֶת־אֲבָנֶיהָ וְאֶת־ עֲפָרָהּ יְחֹנֵנוּ ׃ ¹⁶ וְיִירְאוּ גֹויִם אֶת־ שֵׁם יְהֹוָה וְכָל־מַלְכֵי הָאָרֶץ אֶת־

And *a*mingled my drink with weeping

10 *a*Because of Your indignation and Your wrath,

For You have *b*lifted me up and cast me away.

11 My days are like a [1]*a*lengthened shadow,

And [2]I *b*wither away like [3]grass.

Psa. 102:12 But You, O LORD, [1]*a*abide forever,

And Your [2]*b*name to all generations.

13 You will *a*arise *and* have *b*compassion on Zion;

For *c*it is time to be gracious to her,

For the *d*appointed time has come.

14 Surely Your servants [1]find pleasure in her stones

And feel pity for her dust.

15 [1]So the [2]*a*nations will fear the name of the LORD

And *b*all the kings of the earth Your glory.

16 For the LORD has *a*built up Zion;

He has *b*appeared in His glory.

17 He has *a*regarded the prayer of the [1]destitute

And has not despised their prayer.

Psa. 102:18 [1]This will be *a*written for the *b*generation to come,

[2]That *c*a people yet to be created [3]may praise [4]the LORD.

19 For He *a*looked down from His holy height;

*b*From Heaven the LORD gazed [1]upon the earth,

20 To hear the *a*groaning of the prisoner,

כְּבוֹדֶךָ ׃ 17 כִּי־בָנָה יְהֹוָה צִיּוֹן נִרְאָה בִּכְבוֹדוֹ ׃ 18 פָּנָה אֶל־תְּפִלַּת הָעַרְעָר וְלֹא־בָזָה אֶת־תְּפִלָּתָם ׃ 19 תִּכָּתֶב זֹאת לְדוֹר אַחֲרוֹן וְעַם נִבְרָא יְהַלֶּל־יָהּ ׃ 20 כִּי־הִשְׁקִיף מִמְּרוֹם קָדְשׁוֹ יְהֹוָה מִשָּׁמַיִם אֶל־אֶרֶץ הִבִּיט ׃ 21 לִשְׁמֹעַ אֶנְקַת אָסִיר לְפַתֵּחַ בְּנֵי תְמוּתָה ׃ 22 לְסַפֵּר בְּצִיּוֹן שֵׁם יְהֹוָה וּתְהִלָּתוֹ בִּירוּשָׁלָ͏ִם ׃ 23 בְּהִקָּבֵץ עַמִּים יַחְדָּו וּמַמְלָכוֹת לַעֲבֹד אֶת־יְהֹוָה ׃ 24 עִנָּה בַדֶּרֶךְ כֹּחוֹ [כֹּחִי] קִצַּר יָמָי ׃ 25 אֹמַר אֵלִי אַל־תַּעֲלֵנִי בַּחֲצִי יָמָי בְּדוֹר דּוֹרִים שְׁנוֹתֶיךָ ׃ 26 לְפָנִים הָאָרֶץ יָסַדְתָּ וּמַעֲשֵׂה יָדֶיךָ שָׁמָיִם ׃ 27 הֵמָּה ׀ יֹאבֵדוּ וְאַתָּה תַעֲמֹד וְכֻלָּם כַּבֶּגֶד יִבְלוּ כַּלְּבוּשׁ תַּחֲלִיפֵם וְיַחֲלֹפוּ ׃ 28 וְאַתָּה־הוּא וּשְׁנוֹתֶיךָ לֹא יִתָּמּוּ ׃ 29 בְּנֵי־עֲבָדֶיךָ יִשְׁכּוֹנוּ וְזַרְעָם לְפָנֶיךָ יִכּוֹן ׃

To *b*set free [1]those who were doomed to death,

21 That *men* may *a*tell of the name of the LORD in Zion

And His praise in Jerusalem,

22 When *a*the peoples are gathered together,

And the kingdoms, to serve the LORD.

Psa. 102:23 He has weakened my strength in the way;

He has *a*shortened my days.

24 I say, "O my God, *a*do not take me away in the [1]midst of my days,

Your *b*years are throughout all generations.

25 "Of old You *a*founded the earth,

And the *b*heavens are the work of Your hands.

26 "[1]Even they will *a*perish, but You endure;

And all of them will wear out like a garment;

Like clothing You will change them and they will be changed.

27 "But You are [1]*a*the same,

And Your years will not come to an end.

28 "The *a*children of Your servants will continue,

And their [1]*b*descendants will be established before You."

References

Psalm 102:0
[†]Ps 142:2

Psalm 102:1
[a]Ps 39:12; 61:1
[b]Ex 2:23; 1 Sam 9:16

Psalm 102:2
[a]Ps 69:17
[b]Ps 31:2

Psalm 102:3
[1]Or *finished*
[a]Ps 37:20; James 4:14
[b]Job 30:30; Lam 1:13

Psalm 102:4
[1]Lit *herbage*
[a]Ps 90:5, 6
[b]Ps 37:2; Is 40:7
[c]1 Sam 1:7; 2 Sam 12:17; Ezra 10:6; Job 33:20

Psalm 102:5
[1]Lit *voice*
[2]Lit *have cleaved*
[a]Job 19:20; Lam 4:8

Psalm 102:6
[1]Lit *have become similar to*
[a]Is 34:11; Zeph 2:14

Psalm 102:7
[a]Ps 77:4

Psalm 102:8
[1]Or *made a fool of*
[2]Lit *have sworn by me*

[a]Ps 31:11
[b]Acts 26:11
[c]2 Sam 16:5; Is 65:15; Jer 29:22

Psalm 102:9
[a]Ps 42:3; 80:5

Psalm 102:10
[a]Ps 38:3
[b]Job 27:21; 30:22

Psalm 102:11
[1]Lit *stretched out*
[2]Or *as for me, I*
[3]Lit *herbage*
[a]Job 14:2; Ps 109:23
[b]Ps 102:4

Psalm 102:12
[1]Or *sit enthroned*
[2]Lit *memorial*
[a]Ps 9:7; 10:16; Lam 5:19
[b]Ex 3:15; Ps 135:13

Psalm 102:13
[a]Ps 12:5; 44:26
[b]Is 60:10; Zech 1:12
[c]Ps 119:126
[d]Ps 75:2; Dan 8:19

Psalm 102:14
[1]Or *have found*

Psalm 102:15
[1]Or *And*
[2]Or *Gentiles, heathen*
[a]1 Kin 8:43; Ps 67:7
[b]Ps 138:4

Psalm 102:16
[a]Ps 147:2

[b]Is 60:1, 2

Psalm 102:17
[1]Or *naked*
[a]Neh 1:6; Ps 22:24

Psalm 102:18
[1]Or *Let this be written*
[2]Or *And*
[3]Or *will*
[4]Heb *YAH*
[a]Deut 31:19; Rom 15:4; 1 Cor 10:11
[b]Ps 22:30; 48:13
[c]Ps 22:31; 78:6f

Psalm 102:19
[1]Lit *toward*
[a]Deut 26:15; Ps 14:2; 53:2
[b]Ps 33:13

Psalm 102:20
[1]Lit *the sons of death*
[a]Ps 79:11
[b]Ps 146:7

Psalm 102:21
[a]Ps 22:22

Psalm 102:22
[a]Ps 22:27; 86:9; Is 49:22, 23; 60:3; Zech 8:20-23

Psalm 102:23
[a]Ps 39:5

Psalm 102:24
[1]Lit *half*
[a]Ps 39:13; Is 38:10
[b]Job 36:26; Ps 90:2; 102:12; Hab 1:12

Psalm 102:25
[a]Gen 1:1; Neh 9:6; Heb 1:10-12

[b]Ps 96:5

Psalm 102:26
[1]Lit *They themselves*
[a]Is 34:4; 51:6; Matt 24:35; 2 Pet 3:10; Rev 20:11

Psalm 102:27
[1]Lit *He*
[a]Is 41:4; 43:10; Mal 3:6; James 1:17

Psalm 102:28
[1]Lit *seed*
[a]Ps 69:36
[b]Ps 89:4

Targum

Psa. 102:1 The prayer for the poor man, for he is weary, and will speak his prayer in the presence of the LORD. **2** O LORD, accept my prayer, and let my entreaty come before you. **3** Do not remove your presence from me in the day of my distress; incline your ear unto me; in the day that I call, hasten, answer me. **4** For my days are consumed like smoke; and my limbs burn like an oven. **5** My heart is smitten like grass and will dry up; for I have forgotten the Torah of my instruction. **6** Because of the sound of my groaning, my bones have clung to my flesh. **7** I have become like a marsh-bird in the wilderness; I have become like an owl in the parched land. **8** I stay awake all night, and I have become like a bird that flutters and wanders by itself on the roof. **9** All the day my enemies will jeer at me; those who mock me have sworn by my word in vain. **10** For I have supped on ashes like food, and prepared my drink in weeping. **11** Because of your anger and rage, for you have lifted me up and cast me down. **12** My days are like a shadow that lengthens; and I will wither like grass. **13** But you, O LORD, your dwelling place is eternal, in Heaven you will dwell, and your memorial is to every generation. **14** You will arise, you will pity Zion, for it is time to have compassion on her, for the season has come. **15** For your servants have desired her stones, and they will have mercy on her dust. **16** And the peoples will fear the name of the LORD, and all the kings of the earth your glory. **17** For the city of Zion was built by the command of the LORD, he was revealed in glory. **18** He turned to the prayer of those who were made desolate, and did not despise their prayer. **19** Let this prayer be written for a later generation, and the people yet to be created will praise Yah. **20** For he watched from the high heavens of his holiness; the LORD looked from Heaven to earth. **21** To hear the cry of the prisoners; to set loose the children of those handed over to death. **22** To tell in Zion the name of the LORD, and his praise in Jerusalem. **23** When peoples are gathered together, and kingdoms to worship in the presence of the LORD. **24** My strength is harmed by the weariness of the path of exile; my days are shortened. **25** I will say in the presence of my God, "Do not remove me from the world at the halfway point of my days; bring me to the world to come, because your years are throughout generations of generations." **26** In the beginning when all creatures were created, you founded the earth, and the heavens are the works of your hand. **27** They will perish but you will endure; and all of them like a garment will wear out; like a mantle you will change them and they will pass away. **28** And you are he who created them; and your years do not come to an end. **29** The sons of your servants will abide in the land; and their offspring will be established in your presence.

Spiritual Awareness

Introduction

This Psalm expresses the feelings of the poor enveloped in misery. It describes the state of the people of Israel while in Exile in Babylon. The people were both financially and spiritually poor. They did not receive the generous responses from Heaven that they were used to. There is a sending of hope and redemption at the end of the Psalm.

Verse three

The happiness and independence of the people had been shattered. What is often missed is the people did not have their Temple to the LORD. The Shekinah left the Temple; thus, the presence of the LORD was gone, according to the people. They believed that the LORD resided in the boundaries of the land of Judah. They were in Babylon. How could the LORD find them? They felt this by not being home but also because the LORD did not answer their prayers as part of their punishment.

For my days are consumed like smoke, and my bones are burned as a hearth.

Verse six

The nation's history was filled with ruin and desolation. The people tried to understand why the LORD allowed these things to happen to them. It is easy for people to forget that they were the cause of the problems. For Israel, the Exile came because they were violating the terms of the Sinai Covenant. They were not living by the LORD's Law. When a person says that the LORD is not answering their prayers, they should examine their life to determine if they are following the ways of the LORD.

I am like a bird of the wilderness; I have become like an owl of the waste places.

Notes on the Psalm

The Psalmist moves from the spiritual deprivation of the people into a discourse of how the people will recover. While in Babylon, the people came to understand what they did and did not do. They needed to look at what their behavior was in the past that angered the LORD to bring about the devastation to the nation and especially to Jerusalem. They had to understand it and accept it. The second thing they had to accept was that they were not following the LORD's Law. That is what caused their poor behavior and their problems. Jerusalem was destroyed by the Babylonians, and only some wild animals and nomads lived in the city area. Jerusalem suffered, as did the people. When they turned back to the LORD, they were forgiven for their sins. They were able to return to the land of Judea. When people came to Jerusalem and saw the destruction, they immediately rebuilt the city and the Temple. As the town was rebuilt, their spirituality was rebuilt.

Today, when a person says, "my prayers are not answered," the first thing they should do is examine their life. How well is the person following the LORD's Law? That is the first question that should be asked.

Psalm 103

New American Standard 1995	Hebrew

Psa. 103:0 *A Psalm* of David.
 	
Psa. 103:1 [a]Bless the LORD, O my soul,
   And all that is within me, *bless* His [b]holy name.
2   Bless the LORD, O my soul,
   And [a]forget none of His benefits;
3   Who [a]pardons all your iniquities,
   Who [b]heals all your diseases;
4   Who [a]redeems your life from the pit,
   Who [b]crowns you with lovingkindness and compassion;
5   Who [a]satisfies your [1]years with good things,
   So that your youth is [b]renewed like the eagle.
 	
Psa. 103:6 The LORD [a]performs [1]righteous deeds
   And judgments for all who are [b]oppressed.
7   He [a]made known His ways to Moses,
   His [b]acts to the sons of Israel.
8   The LORD is [a]compassionate and gracious,
   [b]Slow to anger and abounding in lovingkindness.
9   He [a]will not always strive *with us,*
   Nor will He [b]keep *His anger* forever.
10   He has [a]not dealt with us according to our sins,
	לְדָוִד ׀ בָּרֲכִי נַפְשִׁי אֶת־ **Psa. 103:1**
	יְהוָה וְכָל־קְרָבַי אֶת־שֵׁם קָדְשֽׁוֹ ׃ 2
	בָּרֲכִי נַפְשִׁי אֶת־יְהוָה וְאַל־תִּשְׁכְּחִי
	כָּל־גְּמוּלָֽיו ׃ 3 הַסֹּלֵחַ לְכָל־עֲוֹנֵכִי
	הָרֹפֵא לְכָל־תַּחֲלֻאָֽיְכִי ׃ 4 הַגּוֹאֵל
	מִשַּׁחַת חַיָּיְכִי הַֽמְעַטְּרֵכִי חֶסֶד
	וְרַחֲמִֽים ׃ 5 הַמַּשְׂבִּיעַ בַּטּוֹב עֶדְיֵךְ
	תִּתְחַדֵּשׁ כַּנֶּשֶׁר נְעוּרָֽיְכִי ׃ 6 עֹשֵׂה
	צְדָקוֹת יְהוָה וּמִשְׁפָּטִים לְכָל־
	עֲשׁוּקִֽים ׃ 7 יוֹדִיעַ דְּרָכָיו לְמֹשֶׁה
	לִבְנֵי יִשְׂרָאֵל עֲלִילוֹתָֽיו ׃ 8 רַחוּם
	וְחַנּוּן יְהוָה אֶרֶךְ אַפַּיִם וְרַב־חָֽסֶד ׃
	9 לֹא־לָנֶצַח יָרִיב וְלֹא לְעוֹלָם
	יִטּֽוֹר ׃ 10 לֹא כַחֲטָאֵינוּ עָשָׂה לָנוּ
	וְלֹא כַעֲוֹנֹתֵינוּ גָּמַל עָלֵֽינוּ ׃ 11 כִּי
	כִגְבֹהַּ שָׁמַיִם עַל־הָאָרֶץ גָּבַר חַסְדּוֹ
	עַל־יְרֵאָֽיו ׃ 12 כִּרְחֹק מִזְרָח
	מִֽמַּעֲרָב הִרְחִיק מִמֶּנּוּ אֶת־
	פְּשָׁעֵֽינוּ ׃ 13 כְּרַחֵם אָב עַל־בָּנִים
	רִחַם יְהוָה עַל־יְרֵאָֽיו ׃ 14 כִּי־הוּא
	יָדַע יִצְרֵנוּ זָכוּר כִּי־עָפָר אֲנָֽחְנוּ ׃ 15
	אֱנוֹשׁ כֶּחָצִיר יָמָיו כְּצִיץ הַשָּׂדֶה כֵּן
	יָצִֽיץ ׃ 16 כִּי רוּחַ עָבְרָה־בּוֹ וְאֵינֶנּוּ
	וְלֹא־יַכִּירֶנּוּ עוֹד מְקוֹמֽוֹ ׃ 17 וְחֶסֶד

Nor rewarded us according to our iniquities.

11 For as high *a*as the heavens are above the earth,

So great is His lovingkindness toward those who [1]fear Him.

12 As far as the east is from the west,

So far has He *a*removed our transgressions from us.

13 Just *a*as a father has compassion on *his* children,

So the LORD has compassion on those who [1]fear Him.

14 For *a*He Himself knows [1]our frame;

He *b*is mindful that we are *but* *c*dust.

Psa. 103:15 As for man, his days are *a*like grass;

As a *b*flower of the field, so he flourishes.

16 When the *a*wind has passed over it, it is no more,

And its *b*place acknowledges it no longer.

17 But the *a*lovingkindness of the LORD is from everlasting to everlasting on those who [1]fear Him,

And His [2]righteousness *b*to children's children,

18 To *a*those who keep His covenant And remember His precepts to do them.

Psa. 103:19 The LORD has established His *a*throne in the heavens,

And His [1]*b*sovereignty rules over [2]all.

20 Bless the LORD, you *a*His angels,

*b*Mighty in strength, who *c*perform His word,

יְהוָה ׀ מֵעוֹלָם וְעַד־עוֹלָם עַל־
יְרֵאָיו וְצִדְקָתוֹ לִבְנֵי בָנִים ׃ 18
לְשֹׁמְרֵי בְרִיתוֹ וּלְזֹכְרֵי פִקֻּדָיו
לַעֲשׂוֹתָם ׃ 19 יְהוָה בַּשָּׁמַיִם הֵכִין
כִּסְאוֹ וּמַלְכוּתוֹ בַּכֹּל מָשָׁלָה ׃ 20
בָּרֲכוּ יְהוָה מַלְאָכָיו גִּבֹּרֵי כֹחַ עֹשֵׂי
דְבָרוֹ לִשְׁמֹעַ בְּקוֹל דְּבָרוֹ ׃ 21 בָּרֲכוּ
יְהוָה כָּל־צְבָאָיו מְשָׁרְתָיו עֹשֵׂי
רְצוֹנוֹ ׃ 22 בָּרֲכוּ יְהוָה ׀ כָּל־מַעֲשָׂיו
בְּכָל־מְקֹמוֹת מֶמְשַׁלְתּוֹ בָּרֲכִי נַפְשִׁי
אֶת־יְהוָה ׃

<table>
<tr><td>

[d]Obeying the voice of His word!
21 Bless the LORD, all you [a]His hosts,

You [b]who serve Him, doing His will.
22 Bless the LORD, [a]all you works of His,

In all places of His dominion;
Bless the LORD, O my soul!

</td><td>
</td></tr>
</table>

References

Psalm 103:1
[a]Ps 104:1, 35
[b]Ps 33:21; 105:3; 145:21; Ezek 36:21; 39:7

Psalm 103:2
[a]Deut 6:12; 8:11

Psalm 103:3
[a]Ex 34:7; Ps 86:5; 130:8; Is 43:25
[b]Ex 15:26; Ps 30:2; Jer 30:17

Psalm 103:4
[a]Ps 49:15
[b]Ps 5:12

Psalm 103:5
[1]Or *desire*
[a]Ps 107:9; 145:16
[b]Is 40:31

Psalm 103:6
[1]Or *deeds of vindication*
[a]Ps 99:4; 146:7
[b]Ps 12:5

Psalm 103:7
[a]Ex 33:13; Ps 99:7; 147:19
[b]Ps 78:11; 106:22

Psalm 103:8
[a]Ex 34:6; Num 14:18; Neh 9:17; Ps 86:15; Jon 4:2; James 5:11
[b]Ps 145:8; Joel 2:13; Nah 1:3

Psalm 103:9
[a]Ps 30:5; Is 57:16
[b]Jer 3:5, 12; Mic 7:18

Psalm 103:10
[a]Ezra 9:13; Lam 3:22

Psalm 103:11
[1]Or *revere*
[a]Ps 36:5; 57:10

Psalm 103:12
[a]2 Sam 12:13; Is 38:17; 43:25; Zech 3:9; Heb 9:26

Psalm 103:13
[1]Or *revere*
[a]Mal 3:17

Psalm 103:14
[1]I.e. what we are made of
[a]Is 29:16
[b]Ps 78:39
[c]Gen 3:19; Eccl 12:7

Psalm 103:15
[a]Ps 90:5; Is 40:6; 1 Pet 1:24
[b]Job 14:2; James 1:10, 11

Psalm 103:16
[a]Is 40:7
[b]Job 7:10; 8:18; 20:9

Psalm 103:17
[1]Or *revere*
[2]I.e. faithfulness to His gracious promises
[a]Ps 25:6
[b]Ex 20:6; Deut 5:10; Ps 105:8

Psalm 103:18
[a]Deut 7:9; Ps 25:10

Psalm 103:19
[1]Or *kingdom*
[2]I.e. the universe
[a]Ps 11:4

[b]Ps 47:2, 8; Dan 4:17, 25

Psalm 103:20
[a]Ps 148:2
[b]Ps 29:1; 78:25
[c]Matt 6:10
[d]Ps 91:11; Heb 1:14

Psalm 103:21
[a]1 Kin 22:19; Neh 9:6; Ps 148:2; Luke 2:13
[b]Ps 104:4

Psalm 103:22
[a]Ps 145:10

Targum

Psa. 103:1 Composed by David, spoken in prophecy. Bless, O my soul, the name of the LORD, and let all my viscera bless his holy name. [2] Bless, O my soul, the name of the LORD, and do not forget all his nourishment, for he made breasts for your mother instead of insight. [3] Who forgives all your iniquities, who heals all your diseases. [4] Who redeems your life from Gehinnom, who crowned you with kindness and mercy. [5] Who satisfies the days of your old age with goodness, and in the age to come, your youth will be renewed like the eagle of the canopy. [6] The LORD does acts of righteousness, and judgments for all the oppressed. [7] He revealed his ways to Moses, his deeds to the children of Israel. [8] The LORD is merciful and compassionate; he loathes anger and does many deeds of goodness and truth. [9] He will not quarrel always, nor will he retain hostility forever. [10] He has not dealt with us according to our sins, nor has he repaid us according to our iniquities. [11] For as high as the heavens are above the earth, so great is his goodness to those who fear him. [12] As far as the east is from the west, thus far has he removed from us our transgressions. [13] As a father (abba) who loves the children, so the LORD loves those who fear him. [14] For he knows our evil impulse that makes us sin; in his presence it is remembered, for we are from dust. [15] The days of a son of man are like grass; like a blossom of the field, so will he bloom. [16] For a storm-wind has blown on him and he is no more; and he no longer is aware of his place. [17] But the favor of the LORD is upon those that fear him, from this age to the age to come; and his generosity is for the children of [their] children. [18] For those who keep his covenant, and for those who remember his commandments to do them. [19] The LORD has established his throne in the highest heavens; and his kingdom rules over all. [20] Bless the name of the LORD, O his angels, who are mighty in power, who do his word, to obey the sound of his word. [21] Bless the name of the LORD, all his hosts, his ministers who do his will. [22] Bless the name of the LORD, all his works, his dominion is in every place. Bless, O my soul, the name of the LORD.

Spiritual Awareness

Introduction

King David thanked the LORD for His greatest gift – the soul. The soul allows humanity to become a reflection of the sacred heavens, a semblance of the Divine. People often ignore their souls and the true purpose of existence. Too often, the Divine fragment of the soul is overshadowed by the darkness of the flesh. The fundamental lesson of Judaism is to foster an awareness of the Divine soul and to teach humanity how to enhance and enrich the most precious possession so that it will become worthy of standing in the LORD's presence to praise Him.

Verse four

The Sefirah Chesed sends the LORD's lovingkindness to the souls in the grave to raise them to heaven. Through Chesed, the Divine part of the soul is brought back into the Lower Waters of Heaven.

Who redeems your life through Chesed with lovingkindness.

Verse eighteen

As in Psalm 102, an important spiritual lesson is that if a person wants their prayers heard and responded to, they have to live by the LORD's Laws.

To such who keep His covenant to fulfill them

Psalm 104

New American Standard 1995	Hebrew

Psa. 104:1 *a*Bless the LORD, O my soul!

O LORD my God, You are very great;

You are *b*clothed with splendor and majesty,

2   Covering Yourself with *a*light as with a cloak,

*b*Stretching out heaven like a *tent* curtain.

3   [1]He *a*lays the beams of His upper chambers in the waters;

[1]He makes the *b*clouds His chariot;

[1]He walks upon the *c*wings of the wind;

4   [1]He makes [2]*a*the winds His messengers,

[3]Flaming *b*fire His ministers.

Psa. 104:5 He *a*established the earth upon its foundations,

So that it will not [1]totter forever and ever.

6   You *a*covered it with the deep as with a garment;

The waters were standing above the mountains.

7   At Your *a*rebuke they fled,

At the *b*sound of Your thunder they hurried away.

8   The mountains rose; the valleys sank down

To the *a*place which You established for them.

בָּרֲכִי נַפְשִׁי אֶת־יְהוָה **Psa. 104:1**

יְהוָה אֱלֹהַי גָּדַלְתָּ מְּאֹד הוֹד וְהָדָר

לָבָשְׁתָּ ׃ 2 עֹטֶה־אוֹר כַּשַּׂלְמָה נוֹטֶה

שָׁמַיִם כַּיְרִיעָה ׃ 3 הַמְקָרֶה בַמַּיִם

עֲלִיּוֹתָיו הַשָּׂם־עָבִים רְכוּבוֹ

הַמְהַלֵּךְ עַל־כַּנְפֵי־רוּחַ ׃ 4 עֹשֶׂה

מַלְאָכָיו רוּחוֹת מְשָׁרְתָיו אֵשׁ

לֹהֵט ׃ 5 יָסַד־אֶרֶץ עַל־מְכוֹנֶיהָ

בַּל־תִּמּוֹט עוֹלָם וָעֶד ׃ 6 תְּהוֹם

כַּלְּבוּשׁ כִּסִּיתוֹ עַל־הָרִים יַעַמְדוּ־

מָיִם ׃ 7 מִן־גַּעֲרָתְךָ יְנוּסוּן מִן־קוֹל

רַעַמְךָ יֵחָפֵזוּן ׃ 8 יַעֲלוּ הָרִים יֵרְדוּ

בְקָעוֹת אֶל־מְקוֹם זֶה ׀ יָסַדְתָּ

לָהֶם ׃ 9 גְּבוּל־שַׂמְתָּ בַּל־יַעֲבֹרוּן

בַּל־יְשׁוּבוּן לְכַסּוֹת הָאָרֶץ ׃ 10

הַמְשַׁלֵּחַ מַעְיָנִים בַּנְּחָלִים בֵּין

הָרִים יְהַלֵּכוּן ׃ 11 יַשְׁקוּ כָּל־חַיְתוֹ

שָׂדָי יִשְׁבְּרוּ פְרָאִים צְמָאָם ׃ 12

עֲלֵיהֶם עוֹף־הַשָּׁמַיִם יִשְׁכּוֹן מִבֵּין

עֳפָאיִם יִתְּנוּ־קוֹל ׃ 13 מַשְׁקֶה הָרִים

מֵעֲלִיּוֹתָיו מִפְּרִי מַעֲשֶׂיךָ תִּשְׂבַּע

הָאָרֶץ ׃ 14 מַצְמִיחַ חָצִיר ׀ לַבְּהֵמָה

וְעֵשֶׂב לַעֲבֹדַת הָאָדָם לְהוֹצִיא

לֶחֶם מִן־הָאָרֶץ ׃ 15 וְיַיִן ׀ יְשַׂמַּח

[9] You set a [a]boundary that they may not pass over,

So that they will not return to cover the earth.

Psa. 104:10 [1]He sends forth [a]springs in the valleys;

They flow between the mountains;

[11] They [a]give drink to every beast of the field;

The [b]wild donkeys quench their thirst.

[12] [1]Beside them the birds of the heavens [a]dwell;

They [2]lift up *their* voices among the branches.

[13] [1]He [a]waters the mountains from His upper chambers;

[b]The earth is satisfied with the fruit of His works.

Psa. 104:14 [1]He causes the [a]grass to grow for the [2]cattle,

And [b]vegetation for the [3]labor of man,

So that [4]he may bring forth [5]food [c]from the earth,

[15] And [a]wine which makes man's heart glad,

[b]So that he may make *his* face glisten with oil,

And [1]food which [c]sustains man's heart.

[16] The trees of the LORD [1]drink their fill,

The cedars of Lebanon which He planted,

[17] Where the [a]birds build their nests,

And the [b]stork, whose home is the [1]fir trees.

לְבַב־אֱנוֹשׁ לְהַצְהִיל פָּנִים מִשָּׁמֶן
וְלֶחֶם לְבַב־אֱנוֹשׁ יִסְעָד ׃ 16 יִשְׂבְּעוּ
עֲצֵי יְהוָה אַרְזֵי לְבָנוֹן אֲשֶׁר נָטָע ׃
17 אֲשֶׁר־שָׁם צִפֳּרִים יְקַנֵּנוּ חֲסִידָה
בְּרוֹשִׁים בֵּיתָהּ ׃ 18 הָרִים הַגְּבֹהִים
לַיְּעֵלִים סְלָעִים מַחְסֶה לַשְׁפַנִּים ׃ 19
עָשָׂה יָרֵחַ לְמוֹעֲדִים שֶׁמֶשׁ יָדַע
מְבוֹאוֹ ׃ 20 תָּשֶׁת־חֹשֶׁךְ וִיהִי לָיְלָה
בּוֹ־תִרְמֹשׂ כָּל־חַיְתוֹ־יָעַר ׃ 21
הַכְּפִירִים שֹׁאֲגִים לַטָּרֶף וּלְבַקֵּשׁ
מֵאֵל אָכְלָם ׃ 22 תִּזְרַח הַשֶּׁמֶשׁ
יֵאָסֵפוּן וְאֶל־מְעוֹנֹתָם יִרְבָּצוּן ׃ 23
יֵצֵא אָדָם לְפָעֳלוֹ וְלַעֲבֹדָתוֹ עֲדֵי־
עָרֶב ׃ 24 מָה־רַבּוּ מַעֲשֶׂיךָ יְהוָה
כֻּלָּם בְּחָכְמָה עָשִׂיתָ מָלְאָה הָאָרֶץ
קִנְיָנֶךָ ׃ 25 זֶה הַיָּם גָּדוֹל וּרְחַב
יָדַיִם שָׁם־רֶמֶשׂ וְאֵין מִסְפָּר חַיּוֹת
קְטַנּוֹת עִם־גְּדֹלוֹת ׃ 26 שָׁם אֳנִיּוֹת
יְהַלֵּכוּן לִוְיָתָן זֶה־יָצַרְתָּ לְשַׂחֶק־
בּוֹ ׃ 27 כֻּלָּם אֵלֶיךָ יְשַׂבֵּרוּן לָתֵת
אָכְלָם בְּעִתּוֹ ׃ 28 תִּתֵּן לָהֶם יִלְקֹטוּן
תִּפְתַּח יָדְךָ יִשְׂבְּעוּן טוֹב ׃ 29 תַּסְתִּיר
פָּנֶיךָ יִבָּהֵלוּן תֹּסֵף רוּחָם יִגְוָעוּן
וְאֶל־עֲפָרָם יְשׁוּבוּן ׃ 30 תְּשַׁלַּח
רוּחֲךָ יִבָּרֵאוּן וּתְחַדֵּשׁ פְּנֵי אֲדָמָה ׃
31 יְהִי כְבוֹד יְהוָה לְעוֹלָם יִשְׂמַח
יְהוָה בְּמַעֲשָׂיו ׃ 32 הַמַּבִּיט לָאָרֶץ
33 וַתִּרְעָד יִגַּע בֶּהָרִים וְיֶעֱשָׁנוּ ׃

Psa. 104:18   The high mountains are for the *a*wild goats;

The *b*cliffs are a refuge for the [1c]shephanim.

19   He made the moon *a*for the seasons;

The *b*sun knows the place of its setting.

20   You *a*appoint darkness and it becomes night,

In which all the *b*beasts of the forest [1]prowl about.

21   The *a*young lions roar after their prey

[1]And *b*seek their food from God.

22   *When* the sun rises they withdraw And lie down in their *a*dens.

23   Man goes forth to *a*his work And to his labor until evening.

Psa. 104:24   O LORD, how *a*many are Your works!

[1]In *b*wisdom You have made them all;

The *c*earth is full of Your [2]possessions.

25   [1]There is the *a*sea, great and [2]broad,

In which are swarms without number,

Animals both small and great.

26   There the *a*ships move along, *And* [1b]Leviathan, which You have formed to sport in it.

Psa. 104:27   They all *a*wait for You

To *b*give them their food in [1]due season.

28   You give to them, they gather *it* up; You *a*open Your hand, they are satisfied with good.

אָשִׁירָה לַיהוָה בְּחַיָּי אֲזַמְּרָה לֵאלֹהַי בְּעוֹדִי ׃ 34 יֶעֱרַב עָלָיו שִׂיחִי אָנֹכִי אֶשְׂמַח בַּיהוָה ׃ 35 יִתַּמּוּ חַטָּאִים ׀ מִן־הָאָרֶץ וּרְשָׁעִים ׀ עוֹד אֵינָם בָּרֲכִי נַפְשִׁי אֶת־יְהוָה הַלְלוּ־ יָהּ ׃

²⁹ You ^ahide Your face, they are dismayed;

You ^btake away their ¹spirit, they expire

And ^creturn to their dust.

³⁰ You send forth Your ^{1a}Spirit, they are created;

And You renew the face of the ground.

Psa. 104:31 Let the ^aglory of the LORD endure forever;

Let the LORD ^bbe glad in His works;

³² ¹He ^alooks at the earth, and it ^btrembles;

He ^ctouches the mountains, and they smoke.

³³ ¹I will sing to the LORD ^{2a}as long as I live;

¹I will ^bsing praise to my God ³while I have my being.

³⁴ Let my ^ameditation be pleasing to Him;

As for me, I shall ^bbe glad in the LORD.

³⁵ Let sinners be ^aconsumed from the earth

And let the ^bwicked be no more.
^cBless the LORD, O my soul.
^{1d}Praise ²the LORD!

References

Psalm 104:1
[a]Ps 103:22
[b]Ps 93:1

Psalm 104:2
[a]Dan 7:9
[b]Is 40:22

Psalm 104:3
[1]Lit *The one who*
[a]Amos 9:6
[b]Is 19:1
[c]Ps 18:10

Psalm 104:4
[1]Lit *Who*
[2]Or *His angels, spirits*
[3]Or *His ministers flames of fire*
[a]Ps 148:8; Heb 1:7
[b]2 Kin 2:11; 6:17

Psalm 104:5
[1]Or *move out of place*
[a]Job 38:4; Ps 24:2

Psalm 104:6
[a]Gen 1:2

Psalm 104:7
[a]Ps 18:15; 106:9; Is 50:2
[b]Ps 29:3; 77:18

Psalm 104:8
[a]Ps 33:7

Psalm 104:9
[a]Job 38:10, 11; Jer 5:22

Psalm 104:10

[1]Lit *The one who sends*
[a]Ps 107:35; Is 41:18

Psalm 104:11
[a]Ps 104:13
[b]Job 39:5

Psalm 104:12
[1]Or *Over,* Above
[2]Lit *give forth*
[a]Matt 8:20

Psalm 104:13
[1]Lit *Who*
[a]Ps 65:9; 147:8
[b]Jer 10:13

Psalm 104:14
[1]Lit *Who*
[2]Or *beasts*
[3]Or *cultivation by* or *service of*
[4]Or *He*
[5]Lit *bread*
[a]Job 38:27; Ps 147:8
[b]Gen 1:29
[c]Job 28:5

Psalm 104:15
[1]Lit *bread*
[a]Judg 9:13; Prov 31:6; Eccl 10:19
[b]Ps 23:5; 92:10; 141:5; Luke 7:46
[c]Gen 18:5; Judg 19:5, 8

Psalm 104:16
[1]Lit *are satisfied*

Psalm 104:17
[1]Or *cypress*
[a]Ps 104:12
[b]Lev 11:19

Psalm 104:18
[1]Small, shy, furry animals *(Hyrax syriacus)* found in the peninsula of the Sinai, northern Israel, and the region round the Dead Sea; KJV *coney,* orig NASB *rock badgers*
[a]Job 39:1
[b]Prov 30:26
[c]Lev 11:5

Psalm 104:19
[a]Gen 1:14
[b]Ps 19:6

Psalm 104:20
[1]Lit *creep*
[a]Ps 74:16; Is 45:7
[b]Ps 50:10; Is 56:9; Mic 5:8

Psalm 104:21
[1]Lit *And to seek*
[a]Job 38:39
[b]Ps 145:15; Joel 1:20

Psalm 104:22
[a]Job 37:8

Psalm 104:23
[a]Gen 3:19

Psalm 104:24
[1]Or *With*
[2]Or *creatures*
[a]Ps 40:5
[b]Ps 136:5; Prov 3:19; Jer 10:12; 51:15
[c]Ps 65:9

Psalm 104:25
[1]Or *This*
[2]Or *broad of dimensions* (lit *hands*)
[a]Ps 8:8; 69:34

Psalm 104:26
[1]Or *a sea monster*

[a]Ps 107:23; Ezek 27:9
[b]Job 41:1; Ps 74:14; Is 27:1

Psalm 104:27
[1]Lit *its appointed time*
[a]Ps 145:15
[b]Job 36:31; 38:41; Ps 136:25; 147:9

Psalm 104:28
[a]Ps 145:16

Psalm 104:29
[1]Or *breath*
[a]Deut 31:17; Ps 30:7
[b]Job 34:14, 15; Ps 146:4; Eccl 12:7
[c]Gen 3:19; Job 10:9; Ps 90:3

Psalm 104:30
[1]Or *breath*
[a]Job 33:4; Ezek 37:9

Psalm 104:31
[a]Ps 86:12; 111:10
[b]Gen 1:31

Psalm 104:32
[1]Lit *The one who*
[a]Judg 5:5; Ps 97:4, 5; 114:7
[b]Hab 3:10
[c]Ex 19:18; Ps 144:5

Psalm 104:33
[1]Or *Let me sing*
[2]Lit *in my lifetime*
[3]Lit *while I still am*
[a]Ps 63:4
[b]Ps 146:2

Psalm 104:34
[a]Ps 19:14
[b]Ps 9:2

Psalm 104:35
[1]Or *Hallelujah!*
[2]Heb *YAH*
[a]Ps 59:13
[b]Ps 37:10
[c]Ps 104:1
[d]Ps 105:45; 106:48

Targum

Psa. 104:1 Bless, O my soul, the name of the LORD. O LORD my God, you are greatly exalted; you have put on praise and splendor. [2] Who wraps himself in light like a sheet, who stretches out the heavens like a curtain. [3] Who covers his chambers with water like a building with beams; who placed his chariot, as it were, upon swift clouds; who goes on the wings of an eagle. [4] Who made his messengers as swift as wind; his servants, as strong as burning fire. [5] Who lays the foundation of the earth upon its base, so that it will not shake for ages upon ages. [6] You have covered over the abyss as with a garment; and the waters split on the mountains, and endure. [7] At your rebuke, they will flee, flowing down; at the sound of your shout, they will be frightened, pouring themselves out. [8] They will go up from the abyss to the mountains, and descend to the valleys, to this place that you founded for them. [9] You have placed a boundary for the waves of the sea that they will not cross, lest they return to cover the earth. [10] Who releases springs into rivers; they flow between the mountains. [11] They water all the wild animals; the asses will break their thirst. [12] The birds of heaven will settle on them; they will give out a sound of singing from among the branches. [13] Who waters the mountains from his upper treasury; the earth will be satisfied with the fruit of your deeds. [14] Who makes grass grow for beasts, and herbs for the cultivation of the son of man, that bread may come forth from the earth; [15] And wine that gladdens the heart of the son of man, to make the face shine by oil; and bread will support the heart of the son of man. [16] The trees that the LORD created are satisfied, the cedars of Lebanon that he planted: [17] Where the birds make nests; the stork's dwelling is in the cypresses. [18] The high mountains are for the wild goats; the rocks are security for the conies. [19] He made the moon to calculate times by; the sun knows the time of his setting. [20] You will make darkness and it will be night; in it all the beasts of the forest creep about. [21] The offspring of lions roar to find food, and to seek their sustenance from God. [22] The sun will shine, they gather together; and they lay down in their dwelling place. [23] A son of man will go forth to his work and to his cultivation, until the sunset of evening. [24] How many are your works, O LORD! You have made all of them in wisdom; the earth is full of your possessions. [25] This sea is great and broad in extent; creeping things are there without number, both tiny creatures and large. [26] There the ships go about, [and] this Leviathan you created for the sport of the righteous at the supper of his dwelling place. [27] All of them rely on you to give their food in its time. [28] You will give it to them, and they gather it; you will open your hand, and they are satisfied with goodness. [29] You will remove your presence, they are dazed; you will gather their spirit and they expire, and return to their dust. [30] You will send out your holy spirit and they are created; and you will make new the surface of the earth. [31] May the glory of the LORD be eternal; the LORD will rejoice in his works. [32] Who looks at the earth, and it shakes; he draws near to the mountains, and they emit smoke. [33] I will sing praise in the presence of the LORD during my life; I will make music to my God while I exist. [34] May my talk be pleasing in his presence; I will rejoice in the word of the LORD. [35] The sinners will be destroyed from the earth, and wicked exist no longer. Bless, O my soul, the name of the LORD. Hallelujah!

Spiritual Awareness

Introduction

This Psalm is a continuation of the preceding one. David recounts the greatness of the six days of Creation. He speaks about the splendor of the Light of Ein Sof, which created the Sefirot, Heaven, and Earth. The crowning glory of Creation was the creation of humankind. This Psalm is sung on Rosh Chodesh, the first day of the new month.

Notes of this Psalm

In David's day, nothing was taken for granted. He gave thanksgiving to the LORD in several Psalms for all the wonders of Creation. People today tend to take the LORD for granted. Ask yourself, when was the last time you gave thanksgiving to the LORD for the simple things that are usually taken for granted. A pastor offered a thanksgiving prayer before dinner and thanked the LORD for all the components of the dinner, not just the food. He gave thanks for the knives, forks, table, and more. Understanding that everything is a product of the LORD's six days of Creation will make a person humble and grateful before the LORD.

Psalm 105

New American Standard 1995	Hebrew

Psa. 105:1 Oh *a*give thanks to the LORD, *b*call upon His name;

*c*Make known His deeds among the peoples.

2 Sing to Him, *a*sing praises to Him;

1*b*Speak of all His 2wonders.

3 1Glory in His holy name;

Let the *a*heart of those who seek the LORD be glad.

4 Seek the LORD and *a*His strength;

*b*Seek His face continually.

5 Remember His 1*a*wonders which He has done,

His marvels and the *b*judgments 2uttered by His mouth,

6 O seed of *a*Abraham, His servant,

O sons of *b*Jacob, His *c*chosen ones!

7 He is the LORD our God;

His *a*judgments are in all the earth.

Psa. 105:8 He has *a*remembered His covenant forever,

The word which He commanded to a *b*thousand generations,

9 *The* *a*covenant which He made with Abraham,

And His *b*oath to Isaac.

10 Then He *a*confirmed it to Jacob for a statute,

To Israel as an everlasting covenant,

11 Saying, "*a*To you I will give the land of Canaan

As the 1*b*portion of your inheritance,"

הוֹדוּ לַיהוָה קִרְאוּ בִשְׁמוֹ **Psa. 105:1**

הוֹדִיעוּ בָעַמִּים עֲלִילוֹתָיו : 2 שִׁירוּ־

לוֹ זַמְּרוּ־לוֹ שִׂיחוּ בְּכָל־

נִפְלְאוֹתָיו : 3 הִתְהַלְלוּ בְּשֵׁם קָדְשׁוֹ

יִשְׂמַח לֵב | מְבַקְשֵׁי יְהוָה : 4 דִּרְשׁוּ

יְהוָה וְעֻזּוֹ בַּקְּשׁוּ פָנָיו תָּמִיד : 5

זִכְרוּ נִפְלְאוֹתָיו אֲשֶׁר־עָשָׂה מֹפְתָיו

וּמִשְׁפְּטֵי־פִיו : 6 זֶרַע אַבְרָהָם עַבְדּוֹ

בְּנֵי יַעֲקֹב בְּחִירָיו : 7 הוּא יְהוָה

אֱלֹהֵינוּ בְּכָל־הָאָרֶץ מִשְׁפָּטָיו : 8

זָכַר לְעוֹלָם בְּרִיתוֹ דָּבָר צִוָּה

לְאֶלֶף דּוֹר : 9 אֲשֶׁר כָּרַת אֶת־

אַבְרָהָם וּשְׁבוּעָתוֹ לְיִשְׂחָק : 10

וַיַּעֲמִידֶהָ לְיַעֲקֹב לְחֹק לְיִשְׂרָאֵל

בְּרִית עוֹלָם : 11 לֵאמֹר לְךָ אֶתֵּן

אֶת־אֶרֶץ־כְּנָעַן חֶבֶל נַחֲלַתְכֶם : 12

בִּהְיוֹתָם מְתֵי מִסְפָּר כִּמְעַט וְגָרִים

בָּהּ : 13 וַיִּתְהַלְּכוּ מִגּוֹי אֶל־גּוֹי

מִמַּמְלָכָה אֶל־עַם אַחֵר : 14 לֹא־

הִנִּיחַ אָדָם לְעָשְׁקָם וַיּוֹכַח עֲלֵיהֶם

מְלָכִים : 15 אַל־תִּגְּעוּ בִמְשִׁיחָי

וְלִנְבִיאַי אַל־תָּרֵעוּ : 16 וַיִּקְרָא רָעָב

עַל־הָאָרֶץ כָּל־מַטֵּה־לֶחֶם שָׁבָר : 17

שָׁלַח לִפְנֵיהֶם אִישׁ לְעֶבֶד נִמְכַּר

יוֹסֵף : 18 עִנּוּ בַכֶּבֶל רַגְלָיו [רַגְלוֹ]

12 When they were only a *a*few men in number,

Very few, and *b*strangers in it.

13 And they wandered about from nation to nation,

From *one* kingdom to another people.

14 He *a*permitted no man to oppress them,

And He *b*reproved kings for their sakes:

15 "*a*Do not touch My anointed ones,
And do My prophets no harm."

Psa. 105:16 And He *a*called for a famine upon the land;

He *b*broke the whole staff of bread.

17 He *a*sent a man before them,
Joseph, *who* was *b*sold as a slave.

18 They afflicted his *a*feet with fetters,
[1]He himself was laid in irons;

19 Until the time that his *a*word came to pass,

The word of the LORD [1b]tested him.

20 The *a*king sent and released him,
The ruler of peoples, and set him free.

21 He *a*made him lord of his house
And ruler over all his possessions,

22 To [1]imprison his princes [2a]at will,
That he might teach his elders wisdom.

23 *a*Israel also came into Egypt;
Thus Jacob *b*sojourned in the land of Ham.

24 And He *a*caused His people to be very fruitful,

And made them stronger than their adversaries.

בַּרְזֶל בָּאָה נַפְשׁוֹ : ‏19 עַד־עֵת בֹּא־

דְבָרוֹ אִמְרַת יְהוָה צְרָפָתְהוּ : ‏20

שָׁלַח מֶלֶךְ וַיַּתִּירֵהוּ מֹשֵׁל עַמִּים

וַיְפַתְּחֵהוּ : ‏21 שָׂמוֹ אָדוֹן לְבֵיתוֹ

וּמֹשֵׁל בְּכָל־קִנְיָנוֹ : ‏22 לֶאְסֹר שָׂרָיו

בְּנַפְשׁוֹ וּזְקֵנָיו יְחַכֵּם : ‏23 וַיָּבֹא

יִשְׂרָאֵל מִצְרָיִם וְיַעֲקֹב גָּר בְּאֶרֶץ־

חָם : ‏24 וַיֶּפֶר אֶת־עַמּוֹ מְאֹד

וַיַּעֲצִמֵהוּ מִצָּרָיו : ‏25 הָפַךְ לִבָּם

לִשְׂנֹא עַמּוֹ לְהִתְנַכֵּל בַּעֲבָדָיו : ‏26

שָׁלַח מֹשֶׁה עַבְדּוֹ אַהֲרֹן אֲשֶׁר

בָּחַר־בּוֹ : ‏27 שָׂמוּ־בָם דִּבְרֵי אֹתוֹתָיו

וּמֹפְתִים בְּאֶרֶץ חָם : ‏28 שָׁלַח חֹשֶׁךְ

וַיַּחְשִׁךְ וְלֹא־מָרוּ אֶת־דְּבָרוֹ

[דְּבָרוֹ :] ‏29 הָפַךְ אֶת־מֵימֵיהֶם לְדָם

וַיָּמֶת אֶת־דְּגָתָם : ‏30 שָׁרַץ אַרְצָם

צְפַרְדְּעִים בְּחַדְרֵי מַלְכֵיהֶם : ‏31

אָמַר וַיָּבֹא עָרֹב כִּנִּים בְּכָל־

גְּבוּלָם : ‏32 נָתַן גִּשְׁמֵיהֶם בָּרָד אֵשׁ

לֶהָבוֹת בְּאַרְצָם : ‏33 וַיַּךְ גַּפְנָם

וּתְאֵנָתָם וַיְשַׁבֵּר עֵץ גְּבוּלָם : ‏34 אָמַר

וַיָּבֹא אַרְבֶּה וְיֶלֶק וְאֵין מִסְפָּר : ‏35

וַיֹּאכַל כָּל־עֵשֶׂב בְּאַרְצָם וַיֹּאכַל

פְּרִי אַדְמָתָם : ‏36 וַיַּךְ כָּל־בְּכוֹר

בְּאַרְצָם רֵאשִׁית לְכָל־אוֹנָם : ‏37

וַיּוֹצִיאֵם בְּכֶסֶף וְזָהָב וְאֵין בִּשְׁבָטָיו

כּוֹשֵׁל : ‏38 שָׂמַח מִצְרַיִם בְּצֵאתָם

כִּי־נָפַל פַּחְדָּם עֲלֵיהֶם : ‏39 פָּרַשׂ

Psa. 105:25 He [a]turned their heart to hate His people,

To [b]deal craftily with His servants.

26 He [a]sent Moses His servant,

And [b]Aaron, whom He had chosen.

27 They [1a]performed His wondrous acts among them,

And miracles in the land of Ham.

28 He [a]sent darkness and made *it* dark;

And they did not [b]rebel against His words.

29 He [a]turned their waters into blood

And caused their fish to die.

30 Their land swarmed with [a]frogs

Even in the [b]chambers of their kings.

31 He spoke, and there came a [a]swarm of flies

And [b]gnats in all their territory.

32 He [1]gave them [a]hail for rain,

And flaming fire in their land.

33 He [a]struck down their vines also and their fig trees,

And shattered the trees of their territory.

34 He spoke, and [a]locusts came,

And young locusts, even without number,

35 And ate up all vegetation in their land,

And ate up the fruit of their ground.

36 He also [a]struck down all the firstborn in their land,

The [b]first fruits of all their vigor.

Psa. 105:37 Then He brought them out with [a]silver and gold,

עָנָ֣ן לְמָסָ֑ךְ וְ֝אֵ֗שׁ לְהָאִ֥יר לָֽיְלָה׃ [40]

שָׁאַ֣ל וַיָּבֵ֣א שְׂלָ֑ו וְלֶ֥חֶם שָׁ֝מַ֗יִם יַשְׂבִּיעֵֽם׃ [41] פָּ֣תַח צ֭וּר וַיָּז֣וּבוּ מָ֑יִם הָ֝לְכ֗וּ בַּצִּיּ֥וֹת נָהָֽר׃ [42] כִּֽי־זָכַ֗ר אֶת־ [43] דְּבַ֣ר קָדְשׁ֑וֹ אֶֽת־אַבְרָהָ֥ם עַבְדּֽוֹ׃ וַיּוֹצִ֣א עַמּ֣וֹ בְשָׂשׂ֑וֹן בְּ֝רִנָּ֗ה אֶת־ בְּחִירָֽיו׃ [44] וַיִּתֵּ֤ן לָהֶ֗ם אַרְצ֥וֹת גּוֹיִ֑ם וַעֲמַ֖ל לְאֻמִּ֣ים יִירָֽשׁוּ׃ [45] בַּעֲב֤וּר ׀ יִשְׁמְר֣וּ חֻ֭קָּיו וְתוֹרֹתָ֥יו יִנְצֹ֗רוּ הַֽלְלוּ־ יָֽהּ׃

45

And among His tribes there was not one who stumbled.

38 Egypt was *[a]*glad when they departed,

For the *[b]*dread of them had fallen upon them.

39 He spread a *[a]*cloud for a [1]covering,

And *[b]*fire to illumine by night.

40 [1]They *[a]*asked, and He brought *[b]*quail,

And satisfied them with the [2]bread of heaven.

41 He opened the [1]rock and *[a]*water flowed out;

[2]It ran in the dry places *like* a river.

42 For He *[a]*remembered His holy word

With Abraham His servant;

43 And He brought forth His people with joy,

His chosen ones with a joyful *[a]*shout.

44 He *[a]*gave them also the lands of the [1]nations,

That they *[b]*might take possession of *the fruit of* the peoples' labor,

45 So that they might *[a]*keep His statutes

And observe His laws,

[1]Praise [2]the LORD!

References

Psalm 105:1
[a]1 Chr 16:8-22, 34; Ps 106:1; Is 12:4
[b]Ps 99:6
[c]Ps 145:12

Psalm 105:2
[1]Or *Meditate on*
[2]I.e. wonderful acts
[a]Ps 96:1; 98:5
[b]Ps 77:12; 119:27; 145:5

Psalm 105:3
[1]Or *Boast*
[a]Ps 33:21

Psalm 105:4
[a]Ps 63:2
[b]Ps 27:8

Psalm 105:5
[1]I.e. wonderful acts
[2]Lit *of His mouth*
[a]Ps 40:5; 77:11
[b]Ps 119:13

Psalm 105:6
[a]Ps 105:42
[b]Ps 135:4
[c]1 Chr 16:13; Ps 106:5; 135:4

Psalm 105:7
[a]Is 26:9

Psalm 105:8
[a]Ps 105:42; 106:45; Luke 1:72
[b]Deut 7:9

Psalm 105:9
*a*Gen 12:7; 17:2, 8; 22:16-18; Gal 3:17
*b*Gen 26:3

Psalm 105:10
*a*Gen 28:13-15

Psalm 105:11
[1]Lit *measuring line*
*a*Gen 13:15; 15:18
*b*Josh 23:4; Ps 78:55

Psalm 105:12
*a*Gen 34:30; Deut 7:7
*b*Gen 23:4; Heb 11:9

Psalm 105:14
*a*Gen 20:7; 35:5
*b*Gen 12:17; 20:3, 7

Psalm 105:15
*a*Gen 26:11

Psalm 105:16
*a*Gen 41:54
*b*Lev 26:26; Is 3:1; Ezek 4:16

Psalm 105:17
*a*Gen 45:5
*b*Gen 37:28, 36; Acts 7:9

Psalm 105:18
[1]Lit *His soul came into*
*a*Gen 39:20; 40:15

Psalm 105:19
[1]Or *refined*
*a*Gen 40:20, 21
*b*Ps 66:10

Psalm 105:20

[a]Gen 41:14

Psalm 105:21
[a]Gen 41:40-44

Psalm 105:22
[1]Lit *bind*
[2]Lit *at his*
[a]Gen 41:44

Psalm 105:23
[a]Gen 46:6; Acts 7:15
[b]Acts 13:17

Psalm 105:24
[a]Ex 1:7, 9

Psalm 105:25
[a]Ex 1:8; 4:21
[b]Ex 1:10; Acts 7:19

Psalm 105:26
[a]Ex 3:10; 4:12
[b]Ex 4:14; Num 16:5; 17:5-8

Psalm 105:27
[1]Lit *set the words of His signs*
[a]Ps 78:43-51; 105:27-36

Psalm 105:28
[a]Ex 10:21, 22
[b]Ps 99:7

Psalm 105:29
[a]Ex 7:20, 21

Psalm 105:30
[a]Ex 8:6
[b]Ex 8:3

Psalm 105:31

[a]Ex 8:21
[b]Ex 8:16, 17

Psalm 105:32
[1]Or *made their rain hail*
[a]Ex 9:23-25

Psalm 105:33
[a]Ps 78:47

Psalm 105:34
[a]Ex 10:12-15

Psalm 105:36
[a]Ex 12:29; 13:15; Ps 135:8; 136:10
[b]Gen 49:3

Psalm 105:37
[a]Ex 12:35, 36

Psalm 105:38
[a]Ex 12:33
[b]Ex 15:16

Psalm 105:39
[1]Or *curtain*
[a]Ex 13:21; Neh 9:12; Ps 78:14; Is 4:5
[b]Ex 40:38

Psalm 105:40
[1]Or *One*
[2]Or *food*
[a]Ex 16:12; Ps 78:18
[b]Ex 16:13; Num 11:31; Ps 78:27
[c]Ex 16:15; Neh 9:15; Ps 78:24; John 6:31

Psalm 105:41
[1]Or *boulder*
[2]Lit *They went*
[a]Ex 17:6; Num 20:11; Ps 78:15; 114:8; Is 48:21; 1 Cor 10:4

Psalm 105:42
[a]Gen 15:13, 14; Ps 105:8

Psalm 105:43
[a]Ex 15:1; Ps 106:12

Psalm 105:44
[1]Or *Gentiles*
[a]Josh 11:16-23; 13:7; Ps 78:55
[b]Deut 6:10, 11

Psalm 105:45
[1]Or *Hallelujah!*
[2]Heb *YAH*
[a]Deut 4:1, 40

Targum

Psa. 105:1 Sing praise in the presence of the LORD, call on his name; tell of his deeds among the Gentiles. ² Sing praise in his presence, make music in his presence; speak of all his wonders. ³ Sing praise in his holy name; may the heart of those who seek instruction from the presence of the LORD be glad. ⁴ Seek the teaching of the LORD, and his Torah; welcome his face continually. ⁵ Call to mind the wonders that he has done; his miracles, and the judgments of his mouth. ⁶ O seed of Abraham his servant, O sons of Jacob, his chosen ones – ⁷ He is the LORD our God; his judgments are extended over all the earth. ⁸ He remembered his covenant forever; he commanded a word for a thousand generations. ⁹ That which he made with Abraham, and his covenant with Isaac. ¹⁰ And he established it for Jacob as a decree, for Israel as a perpetual covenant. ¹¹ Saying, "To you I will give the land of Canaan as the lot of your inheritance." ¹² When you were a people few in number, like little ones, and dwelling in it. ¹³ And they went from people to people, from one kingdom to [another people.] ¹⁴ He did not allow anyone to oppress them, and he rebuked kings on their account. ¹⁵ Do not come near my anointed ones, and do no harm to my prophets. ¹⁶ And he proclaimed a famine against the land; he broke every support of food. ¹⁷ He sent a wise man before them; Joseph was sold as a slave. ¹⁸ They afflicted his feet with chains; a collar of iron went on his soul. ¹⁹ Until the time when his word came true; the word of the LORD purified him. ²⁰ He sent a king and freed him; a ruler of peoples, and he set him free. ²¹ He made him master of his house, and ruler of all his property. ²² To bind his princes to, as it were, his soul; and he grew wiser than his elders. ²³ And Israel came to Egypt, and Jacob dwelt in the land of Ham. ²⁴ And he made his people very numerous, and made it stronger than its oppressors. ²⁵ Their heart was changed to hate his people, to plot evil things against his servants. ²⁶ He sent Moses his servant, Aaron, with whom he was pleased. ²⁷ They set among them the decrees of his signs, and wonders in the land of Ham. ²⁸ He sent darkness and darkened them, and they did not rebel against his word. ²⁹ He turned their water into blood, and killed all their fish. ³⁰ Their land crawled with frogs in the chambers of their kings. ³¹ He spoke, and brought swarms, vermin in all their territory. ³² He gave their rain as hail, blazing fire in their land. ³³ And he smote their vines and their figs, and smashed the trees of their territory. ³⁴ He spoke, and brought locusts, and grasshoppers without number. ³⁵ And they obliterated all the grass in their land, and consumed the fruits of their land. ³⁶ And he smote every firstborn in Egypt, the beginning of all their strength. ³⁷ And he brought them out with silver and with gold, and they did not quarrel with the Egyptians about the weight. ³⁸ The Egyptians rejoiced when they left, for fear of them had fallen upon them. ³⁹ He spread out the clouds like a curtain, and fire to give light at night. ⁴⁰ They asked for flesh and he brought quail; and he will satisfy them with the bread of heaven. ⁴¹ He opened the rock and water flowed; it went into the dry places like a river. ⁴² For he remembered his holy utterance with Abraham his servant. ⁴³ And he brought out his people in joy, his chosen ones with praise. [44] And he gave to them the lands of the Gentiles; and they will inherit the labor of the peoples. [45] In order that they might keep his ordinances, and observe his Torah. Hallelujah!

Spiritual Awareness

Introduction

This Psalm was composed on the day King David brought the Ark of the Covenant from its temporary location in the home of Oved Edon to the holy city of Jerusalem. There was a lavish ceremony that day for the LORD. The Psalmist emphasizes that the Jews who escorted the Ark were the children of Abraham. Abraham's greatest accomplishment was traveling from place to place, teaching the Name of the One God, the LORD. The Ark represents the name of the LORD. When David carried the Ark from place to place, he resembled his illustrious forebear Abraham.

Verse three

Seeking your glory in the name of the LORD is done by persons who want to follow the ways of the Torah

Seek your glory in His Holy Name, so that the heart of those that seek God may rejoice.

Notes on this Psalm

It seems today that young people generally do not care about history. That is sad because it is through the historical record that a person finds the works of the LORD. Judaism is a religion dedicated to the LORD because of the nation's history. This Psalm highlights Israel's national history. Throughout her history, one can find the LORD at work. Secular Jews have also forgotten this. The children of Abraham became the Chosen people of the LORD because of the events in Egypt and Mount Sinai. The Passover cements the future generations of Jews to the LORD. A Midrash says that all Jewish souls came into the valley at Mount Sinai when the LORD presented the Ten Commandments and the Torah. The LORD asked whether the souls would abide by the Torah. In exchange, the LORD said he would always be with the people. These people were the only Earth nation willing to accept the LORD's protection in exchange for the Torah.

History proves that when the nation followed the Torah, the LORD protected them and gave them prosperity. When the country violated the Torah, the LORD's anger was the removal of His protection. As long as a Jew tries to live by the Torah, the LORD will always be with the person. This understanding has been expressed in prior Psalms. For the Jew, the dedication to the LORD is through history first and personal experiences second. It is the greatest honor to say that one belongs to the Chosen People.

Other nations are invited to partake in the LORD's grace by accepting the Torah. Unfortunately, in most cases, the Goyim have decided to punish the nation of Israel by persecuting the Children of Abraham, whether they happen to be living. Human history would be less bloody if the Goyim accepted the LORD.

The Christian Messiah Yeshua brought this message to the Jews under Roman persecution. He told them to repent! That meant going back to living by the Torah. Many did so, and many followed Yeshua to learn from him how to live by the Torah in their world. Today one can find ways to follow the LORD's Torah through the words and acts of Yeshua of Nazareth. Sadly, Yeshua churches have so many antisemitic members. They have distorted Yeshua of Nazareth's teaching into a form that allowed the Christian Church to take over most of Europe for centuries. The backlash from the Church's control of Europe is still being seen today. Yeshua did not want to create a new religion. He wanted his Jewish brothers and sisters to return to Torah living. The second part of his mission was to bring the Gentiles into the Kingdom of Heaven, which meant they would also follow the Torah.

57

Psalm 106

New American Standard 1995	Hebrew
Psa. 106:1 [1]Praise [2]the LORD! Oh [a]give thanks to the LORD, for He [b]is good; For [c]His lovingkindness is everlasting. [2] Who can speak of the [a]mighty deeds of the LORD, Or can show forth all His praise? [3] How blessed are those who keep [1]justice, [2]Who [a]practice righteousness at all times! **Psa. 106:4** Remember me, O LORD, in *Your* [a]favor [1]toward Your people; Visit me with Your salvation, [5] That I may see the [a]prosperity of Your chosen ones, That I may [b]rejoice in the gladness of Your nation, That I may [c]glory with Your [1]inheritance. **Psa. 106:6** [a]We have sinned [1][b]like our fathers, We have committed iniquity, we have behaved wickedly. [7] Our fathers in Egypt did not understand Your [1]wonders; They [a]did not remember [2]Your abundant kindnesses, But [b]rebelled by the sea, at the [3]Red Sea. [8] Nevertheless He saved them [a]for the sake of His name,	הַלְלוּיָהּ ׀ הוֹדוּ לַיהוָה כִּי־ **Psa. 106:1** טוֹב כִּי לְעוֹלָם חַסְדּוֹ ׃ ² מִי יְמַלֵּל גְּבוּרוֹת יְהוָה יַשְׁמִיעַ כָּל־תְּהִלָּתוֹ ׃ ³ אַשְׁרֵי שֹׁמְרֵי מִשְׁפָּט עֹשֵׂה צְדָקָה בְכָל־עֵת ׃ ⁴ זָכְרֵנִי יְהוָה בִּרְצוֹן עַמֶּךָ פָּקְדֵנִי בִּישׁוּעָתֶךָ ׃ ⁵ לִרְאוֹת ׀ בְּטוֹבַת בְּחִירֶיךָ לִשְׂמֹחַ בְּשִׂמְחַת גּוֹיֶךָ לְהִתְהַלֵּל עִם־נַחֲלָתֶךָ ׃ ⁶ חָטָאנוּ עִם־אֲבוֹתֵינוּ הֶעֱוִינוּ הִרְשָׁעְנוּ ׃ ⁷ אֲבוֹתֵינוּ בְמִצְרַיִם ׀ לֹא־הִשְׂכִּילוּ נִפְלְאוֹתֶיךָ לֹא זָכְרוּ אֶת־רֹב חֲסָדֶיךָ וַיַּמְרוּ עַל־יָם בְּיַם־ סוּף ׃ ⁸ וַיּוֹשִׁיעֵם לְמַעַן שְׁמוֹ לְהוֹדִיעַ אֶת־גְּבוּרָתוֹ ׃ ⁹ וַיִּגְעַר בְּיַם־סוּף וַיֶּחֱרָב וַיּוֹלִיכֵם בַּתְּהֹמוֹת כַּמִּדְבָּר ׃ ¹⁰ וַיּוֹשִׁיעֵם מִיַּד שׂוֹנֵא וַיִּגְאָלֵם מִיַּד אוֹיֵב ׃ ¹¹ וַיְכַסּוּ־מַיִם צָרֵיהֶם אֶחָד מֵהֶם לֹא נוֹתָר ׃ ¹² וַיַּאֲמִינוּ בִדְבָרָיו יָשִׁירוּ תְּהִלָּתוֹ ׃ ¹³ מִהֲרוּ שָׁכְחוּ מַעֲשָׂיו לֹא־חִכּוּ לַעֲצָתוֹ ׃ ¹⁴ וַיִּתְאַוּוּ תַאֲוָה בַּמִּדְבָּר וַיְנַסּוּ־אֵל בִּישִׁימוֹן ׃ ¹⁵ וַיִּתֵּן לָהֶם שֶׁאֱלָתָם וַיְשַׁלַּח רָזוֹן בְּנַפְשָׁם ׃ ¹⁶ וַיְקַנְאוּ לְמֹשֶׁה בַּמַּחֲנֶה לְאַהֲרֹן

That He might *make His power known.

9 Thus He *rebuked the ¹Red Sea and it *dried up,

And He ʿled them through the deeps, as through the wilderness.

10 So He *saved them from the ¹hand of the one who hated *them*,

And *redeemed them from the ¹hand of the enemy.

11 *The waters covered their adversaries;

Not one of them was left.

12 Then they *believed His words; They *sang His praise.

Psa. 106:13 They quickly *forgot His works;

They *did not wait for His counsel,

14 But *craved intensely in the wilderness,

And ¹*tempted God in the desert.

15 So He *gave them their request,

But *sent a ¹wasting disease among them.

Psa. 106:16 When they became *envious of Moses in the camp,

And of Aaron, the holy one of the LORD,

17 The *earth opened and swallowed up Dathan,

And engulfed the ¹company of Abiram.

18 And a *fire blazed up in their ¹company;

The flame consumed the wicked.

Psa. 106:19 They *made a calf in Horeb

And worshiped a molten image.

קָדוֹשׁ יְהֹוָה : ¹⁷ תִּפְתַּח־אֶרֶץ וַתִּבְלַע דָּתָן וַתְּכַס עַל־עֲדַת אֲבִירָם : ¹⁸ וַתִּבְעַר־אֵשׁ בַּעֲדָתָם לֶהָבָה תְּלַהֵט רְשָׁעִים : ¹⁹ יַעֲשׂוּ־ עֵגֶל בְּחֹרֵב וַיִּשְׁתַּחֲווּ לְמַסֵּכָה : ²⁰ וַיָּמִירוּ אֶת־כְּבוֹדָם בְּתַבְנִית שׁוֹר אֹכֵל עֵשֶׂב : ²¹ שָׁכְחוּ אֵל מוֹשִׁיעָם עֹשֶׂה גְדֹלוֹת בְּמִצְרָיִם : ²² נִפְלָאוֹת בְּאֶרֶץ חָם נוֹרָאוֹת עַל־יַם־סוּף : ²³ וַיֹּאמֶר לְהַשְׁמִידָם לוּלֵי מֹשֶׁה בְחִירוֹ עָמַד בַּפֶּרֶץ לְפָנָיו לְהָשִׁיב חֲמָתוֹ מֵהַשְׁחִית : ²⁴ וַיִּמְאֲסוּ בְּאֶרֶץ חֶמְדָּה לֹא־הֶאֱמִינוּ לִדְבָרוֹ : ²⁵ וַיֵּרָגְנוּ בְאָהֳלֵיהֶם לֹא שָׁמְעוּ בְּקוֹל יְהֹוָה : ²⁶ וַיִּשָּׂא יָדוֹ לָהֶם לְהַפִּיל אוֹתָם בַּמִּדְבָּר : ²⁷ וּלְהַפִּיל זַרְעָם בַּגּוֹיִם וּלְזָרוֹתָם בָּאֲרָצוֹת : ²⁸ וַיִּצָּמְדוּ לְבַעַל פְּעוֹר וַיֹּאכְלוּ זִבְחֵי מֵתִים : ²⁹ וַיַּכְעִיסוּ בְּמַעַלְלֵיהֶם וַתִּפְרָץ־בָּם מַגֵּפָה : ³⁰ וַיַּעֲמֹד פִּינְחָס וַיְפַלֵּל וַתֵּעָצַר הַמַּגֵּפָה : ³¹ וַתֵּחָשֶׁב לוֹ לִצְדָקָה לְדֹר וָדֹר עַד־ עוֹלָם : ³² וַיַּקְצִיפוּ עַל־מֵי מְרִיבָה וַיֵּרַע לְמֹשֶׁה בַּעֲבוּרָם : ³³ כִּי־הִמְרוּ אֶת־רוּחוֹ וַיְבַטֵּא בִּשְׂפָתָיו : ³⁴ לֹא־ הִשְׁמִידוּ אֶת־הָעַמִּים אֲשֶׁר אָמַר יְהֹוָה לָהֶם : ³⁵ וַיִּתְעָרְבוּ בַגּוֹיִם וַיִּלְמְדוּ מַעֲשֵׂיהֶם : ³⁶ וַיַּעַבְדוּ אֶת־

20 Thus they *exchanged their glory
For the image of an ox that eats grass.

21 They *forgot God their Savior,
Who had done *great things in Egypt,

22 [1]*Wonders in the land of Ham
And awesome things by the [2]Red Sea.

23 Therefore *He said that He would destroy them,
Had not *Moses His chosen one stood in the breach before Him,
To turn away His wrath from destroying *them.*

24 Then they *despised the *pleasant land;
They *did not believe in His word,

25 But *grumbled in their tents;
They did not listen to the voice of the LORD.

26 Therefore He [1]*swore to them
That He would cast them down in the wilderness,

27 And that He would *cast their seed among the nations
And *scatter them in the lands.

Psa. 106:28 They *joined themselves also to [1]Baal-peor,
And ate *sacrifices offered to the dead.

29 Thus they *provoked *Him* to anger with their deeds,
And the plague broke out among them.

30 Then Phinehas *stood up and interposed,
And so the *plague was stayed.

31 And it was *reckoned to him for righteousness,

עֲצַבֵּיהֶם וַיִּהְיוּ לָהֶם לְמוֹקֵשׁ ׃ 37
וַיִּזְבְּחוּ אֶת־בְּנֵיהֶם וְאֶת־בְּנוֹתֵיהֶם
לַשֵּׁדִים ׃ 38 וַיִּשְׁפְּכוּ דָם נָקִי דַּם־
בְּנֵיהֶם וּבְנוֹתֵיהֶם אֲשֶׁר זִבְּחוּ
לַעֲצַבֵּי כְנַעַן וַתֶּחֱנַף הָאָרֶץ
בַּדָּמִים ׃ 39 וַיִּטְמְאוּ בְמַעֲשֵׂיהֶם וַיִּזְנוּ
בְּמַעַלְלֵיהֶם ׃ 40 וַיִּחַר־אַף יְהוָה
בְּעַמּוֹ וַיְתָעֵב אֶת־נַחֲלָתוֹ ׃ 41 וַיִּתְּנֵם
בְּיַד־גּוֹיִם וַיִּמְשְׁלוּ בָהֶם שֹׂנְאֵיהֶם ׃
42 וַיִּלְחָצוּם אוֹיְבֵיהֶם וַיִּכָּנְעוּ תַּחַת
יָדָם ׃ 43 פְּעָמִים רַבּוֹת יַצִּילֵם וְהֵמָּה
יַמְרוּ בַעֲצָתָם וַיָּמֹכּוּ בַּעֲוֹנָם ׃ 44
וַיַּרְא בַּצַּר לָהֶם בְּשָׁמְעוֹ אֶת־
רִנָּתָם ׃ 45 וַיִּזְכֹּר לָהֶם בְּרִיתוֹ וַיִּנָּחֶם
כְּרֹב חֲסָדוֹ [חַסְדָּיו ׃] 46 וַיִּתֵּן אוֹתָם
לְרַחֲמִים לִפְנֵי כָּל־שׁוֹבֵיהֶם ׃ 47
הוֹשִׁיעֵנוּ ׀ יְהוָה אֱלֹהֵינוּ וְקַבְּצֵנוּ
מִן־הַגּוֹיִם לְהֹדוֹת לְשֵׁם קָדְשֶׁךָ
לְהִשְׁתַּבֵּחַ בִּתְהִלָּתֶךָ ׃ 48 בָּרוּךְ־
יְהוָה אֱלֹהֵי יִשְׂרָאֵל מִן־הָעוֹלָם ׀
וְעַד הָעוֹלָם וְאָמַר כָּל־הָעָם אָמֵן
הַלְלוּ־יָהּ ׃

To all generations forever.

Psa. 106:32   They also *a*provoked *Him* to wrath at the waters of [1]Meribah,

So that it *b*went hard with Moses on their account;

[33]   Because they *a*were rebellious against [1]His Spirit,

He spoke rashly with his lips.

Psa. 106:34   They *a*did not destroy the peoples,

As *b*the LORD commanded them,

[35]   But *a*they mingled with the nations And learned their [1]practices,

[36]   And *a*served their idols, *b*Which became a snare to them.

[37]   They even *a*sacrificed their sons and their daughters to the *b*demons,

[38]   And shed *a*innocent blood, The blood of their *b*sons and their daughters,

Whom they sacrificed to the idols of Canaan;

And the land was *c*polluted with the blood.

[39]   Thus they became *a*unclean in their [1]practices,

And *b*played the harlot in their deeds.

Psa. 106:40   Therefore the *a*anger of the LORD was kindled against His people

And He *b*abhorred His [1c]inheritance.

[41]   Then *a*He gave them into the hand of the [1]nations,

And those who hated them ruled over them.

42 Their enemies also *a*oppressed them,
  And they were subdued under their [1]power.
43 Many times He would *a*deliver them;
  They, however, were rebellious in their *b*counsel,
  And *so* *c*sank down in their iniquity.

Psa. 106:44 Nevertheless He looked upon their distress
  When He *a*heard their cry;
45 And He *a*remembered His covenant for their sake,
  And [1b]relented *c*according to the greatness of His lovingkindness.
46 He also made them *a*objects* of compassion
  In the presence of all their captors.

Psa. 106:47 *a*Save us, O LORD our God,
  And *b*gather us from among the nations,
  To give thanks to Your holy name
  And [1c]glory in Your praise.
48 *a*Blessed be the LORD, the God of Israel,
  From everlasting even to everlasting.
  And let all the people say, "Amen."
  [1]Praise [2]the LORD!

References

Psalm 106:1
[1]Or *Hallelujah!*
[2]Heb *YAH*
[a]Ps 105:1; 107:1; 118:1; 136:1; Jer 33:11
[b]2 Chr 5:13; 7:3; Ezra 3:11; Ps 100:5
[c]1 Chr 16:34, 41

Psalm 106:2
[a]Ps 145:4, 12; 150:2

Psalm 106:3
[1]Or *judgment*
[2]Many Heb mss read *The one who performs*
[a]Ps 15:2

Psalm 106:4
[1]Lit *of*
[a]Ps 44:3; 119:132

Psalm 106:5
[1]I.e. people
[a]Ps 1:3
[b]Ps 118:15
[c]Ps 105:3

Psalm 106:6
[1]Lit *with*
[a]1 Kin 8:47; Ezra 9:7; Neh 1:7; Jer 3:25; Dan 9:5
[b]2 Chr 30:7; Neh 9:2; Ps 78:8, 57; Zech 1:4

Psalm 106:7
[1]I.e. wonderful acts
[2]Lit *the multitude of Your lovingkindnesses*
[3]Lit *Sea of Reeds*
[a]Judg 3:7; Ps 78:11, 42
[b]Ex 14:11, 12; Ps 78:17

Psalm 106:8

[a]Ezek 20:9
[b]Ex 9:16

Psalm 106:9
[1]Lit *Sea of Reeds*
[a]Ps 18:15; 78:13; Is 50:2; Nah 1:4
[b]Ex 14:21; Is 51:10
[c]Is 63:11-13

Psalm 106:10
[1]Or *power*
[a]Ex 14:30
[b]Ps 78:42; 107:2

Psalm 106:11
[a]Ex 14:27, 28; 15:5; Ps 78:53

Psalm 106:12
[a]Ex 14:31
[b]Ex 15:1-21; Ps 105:43

Psalm 106:13
[a]Ex 15:24; 16:2; 17:2
[b]Ps 107:11

Psalm 106:14
[1]Or *put God to the test*
[a]Num 11:4; Ps 78:18; 1 Cor 10:6
[b]Ex 17:2; 1 Cor 10:9

Psalm 106:15
[1]Or *leanness into their soul*
[a]Num 11:31; Ps 78:29
[b]Is 10:16

Psalm 106:16
[a]Num 16:1-3

Psalm 106:17
[1]Or *assembly, band*
[a]Num 16:32; Deut 11:6

Psalm 106:18
[1]Or *assembly, band*
[a]Num 16:35

Psalm 106:19
[a]Ex 32:4; Deut 9:8; Acts 7:41

Psalm 106:20
[a]Jer 2:11; Rom 1:23

Psalm 106:21
[a]Ps 78:11; 106:7, 13
[b]Deut 10:21

Psalm 106:22
[1]I.e. Wonderful acts
[2]Lit *Sea of Reeds*
[a]Ps 105:27

Psalm 106:23
[a]Ex 32:10; Deut 9:14; Ezek 20:8, 13
[b]Ex 32:11-14; Deut 9:25-29

Psalm 106:24
[a]Num 14:31
[b]Deut 8:7; Jer 3:19; Ezek 20:6
[c]Deut 1:32; 9:23; Heb 3:19

Psalm 106:25
[a]Num 14:2; Deut 1:27

Psalm 106:26
[1]Lit *lifted up His hand*
[a]Num 14:28-35; Ps 95:11; Ezek 20:15; Heb 3:11

Psalm 106:27
[a]Deut 4:27
[b]Lev 26:33; Ps 44:11

Psalm 106:28

[1]Or *Baal of Peor*
[a]Num 25:3; Deut 4:3; Hos 9:10
[b]Num 25:2

Psalm 106:29
[a]Num 25:4

Psalm 106:30
[a]Num 25:7
[b]Num 25:8

Psalm 106:31
[a]Gen 15:6; Num 25:11-13

Psalm 106:32
[1]Lit *strife*
[a]Num 20:2-13; Ps 81:7; 95:9
[b]Num 20:12

Psalm 106:33
[1]Or *his spirit*
[a]Num 20:3, 10; Ps 78:40; 107:11

Psalm 106:34
[a]Judg 1:21, 27-36
[b]Deut 7:2, 16

Psalm 106:35
[1]Lit *works*
[a]Judg 3:5, 6

Psalm 106:36
[a]Judg 2:12
[b]Deut 7:16

Psalm 106:37
[a]Deut 12:31; 32:17; 2 Kin 16:3; 17:17; Ezek 16:20, 21; 1 Cor 10:20
[b]Lev 17:7

Psalm 106:38
[a]Ps 94:21

[b]Deut 18:10
[c]Num 35:33; Is 24:5; Jer 3:1, 2

Psalm 106:39
[1]Lit *works*
[a]Lev 18:24; Ezek 20:18
[b]Lev 17:7; Num 15:39; Judg 2:17; Hos 4:12

Psalm 106:40
[1]I.e. people
[a]Judg 2:14; Ps 78:59
[b]Lev 26:30; Deut 32:19
[c]Deut 9:29; 32:9

Psalm 106:41
[1]Or *Gentiles*
[a]Judg 2:14; Neh 9:27

Psalm 106:42
[1]Lit *hand*
[a]Judg 4:3; 10:12

Psalm 106:43
[a]Judg 2:16-18
[b]Ps 81:12
[c]Judg 6:6

Psalm 106:44
[a]Judg 3:9; 6:7; 10:10

Psalm 106:45
[1]Lit *was sorry*
[a]Lev 26:42; Ps 105:8
[b]Judg 2:18
[c]Ps 69:16

Psalm 106:46
[a]1 Kin 8:50; 2 Chr 30:9; Ezra 9:9; Neh 1:11; Jer 42:12

Psalm 106:47
[1]Lit *boast*

[a]1 Chr 16:35, 36
[b]Ps 147:2
[c]Ps 47:1

Psalm 106:48
[1]Or *Hallelujah!*
[2]Heb *YAH*
[a]Ps 41:13; 72:18; 89:52

Targum

Psa. 106:1 Hallelujah! Give thanks in the presence of the LORD, for he is good, for his goodness is forever. **2** Who is able to utter the might of the LORD? [Who] is allowed to proclaim all his praises? **3** Happy are they who observe judgment, those who do righteousness at every time. **4** Remember me, O LORD, with good will toward your people; call me to mind with your redemption. **5** To look on the plenty of your chosen ones; to rejoice in the joy of your people; to join in praise with your inheritance. **6** We have sinned, along with our fathers; we have committed iniquity, acted wickedly. **7** Our fathers in Egypt paid no heed to your wonders; they did not call to mind your great goodness; and they rebelled against your word by the sea, at the Sea of Reeds. **8** And he redeemed them for his name's sake, to make known his might. **9** And he rebuked the Sea of Reeds, and it dried up; and he conducted them through the deeps, as in the wilderness. **10** And he redeemed them from the power of the foe; and he redeemed them from the power of the enemies. **11** And the waters covered their oppressors; not one of them was left. **12** And they believed in the name of his word; they sang his praise. **13** They quickly forgot his deeds; they did not wait for his counsel. **14** And they made a request and tested God in the place of desolation. **15** And he gave them their request, and sent leanness into their souls. **16** And they were jealous of Moses in the camp, of Aaron, the holy one of the LORD. **17** The earth opened up and swallowed Dathan, and covered the company of Abiram. **18** And fire burned in their company; flame will kindle the wicked. **19** They made a calf in Horeb, and bowed down to something of metal. **20** And they exchanged the glory of their master for the likeness of a bull that eats grass and befouls itself. **21** They forgot God their redeemer who had done mighty works in Egypt. **22** Wonders in the land of Ham, awesome things by the Sea of Reeds. **23** And he commanded by his word to destroy them, had it not been for Moses his chosen one, who stood and grew mighty in prayer in his presence to turn aside his wrath from obliteration. **24** And their soul was repelled by the desirable land; they did not believe his word. **25** And they complained in their tents; they did not accept the word of the LORD. **26** And he lifted his hand in an oath because of them, to throw them down slain in the wilderness. **27** And to exile their seed among the peoples, and to scatter them among the lands. **28** And they attached themselves to the idol of Peor, and they ate the sacrifices of the dead. **29** And they caused anger in his presence by their deeds, and plague attacked them. **30** And Phinehas rose and prayed, and the plague was restrained. **31** And it was accounted to him for merit for all generations forever. **32** And they caused anger by the waters of Dispute, and it grieved Moses because of them. **33** For they rebelled against his holy spirit, and he had explained [it] clearly with his lips. **34** They did not destroy the peoples, which the LORD had commanded them [to do]. **35** And they mingled with the Gentiles and they learned their deeds. **36** And they worshipped their idol, and they became a stumbling-block for them. **37** And they sacrificed their sons and their daughters to the demons. **38** And they shed innocent blood – the blood of their sons and daughters that they sacrificed to the idols of the Canaanites – and the land was defiled by capital crimes. [39] And brought uncleanness by their deeds and went astray by their acts. [40] And the anger of the LORD was harsh against his people and he despised his inheritance. [41] And he handed them over into the power of the Gentiles, and their foes ruled over them. [42] And their enemies oppressed them, and they were subdued under their hand. [43] Many times he would deliver them, but they would rebel against him in their counsel, and they were brought low in their sins. [44] And he saw when it went ill with them, when he heard their prayer. [45] And he remembered his covenant in their favor, and he turned aside from his anger according to his abundant mercies. [46] And he made them find mercy in the sight of all who had taken them captive. [47] Redeem us, O LORD our God, and gather us from among the Gentiles, to give thanks in your holy name, to boast in your praise. [48] Blessed be the name of the LORD God of Israel, from this age to the age to come, and let all the people say, Amen, Hallelujah.

Spiritual Awareness

Introduction

This Psalm continues the narrative from Psalm 105. The Psalmist wrote about how the LORD sustained the Jews as they wandered in the wilderness for forty years. While the LORD displayed his unprecedented kindness to Israel, the people neglected their duty to the LORD. They rebelled against Moses and Aaron, which initiated their moral and ethical decline, eventually leading to the Babylonian Exile.

Verse four

Every person must remember that they are responsible for their duties to the LORD. One's loyalty must always be to the LORD. In addition, they must remember that they are a Jewish community member.

Remember me, O LORD, in the favor You extend to Your people; O think of me at Your salvation.

Notes on the Psalm

Taking the LORD for granted happened in Israel's past and still happens today. One of the obligations is to serve the LORD in some capacity. In the Christian Scriptures, Saint Paul wrote that every person contributes some God-given talent to the community. The same holds true in the Hebrew Scriptures. Every member of the community contributes something unique to the person. Part of the covenant with the LORD is to study the Scriptures. Clearly, today this is not an imperative in most communities. Whether it is the synagogue or church, the attendance and participation of people are declining rapidly. US society has been under pressure to remove God from all aspects of life, and the woke have become very good at it. Part of their success is that people who say they are God-fearing really are not. They are not reading and studying their Bible. They are not attending synagogues and church worship events.

Apathy has invaded religious life in the US and this is destroying God worship. During the Covid pandemic political leaders had no problem shutting down churches. Even church bishops begged churches to shutdown. This exasberated the problem causing even more decline. Apathy can set in quickly once the "habit" of attending worship celebrations is broken. The motto "in God we trust" which is on US currency will probably be attacked next and the woke might win. How can God serving people fight back when their numbers are so small.

Eventually the LORD will intervene into our society. The LORD sent the Babylonians to Jerusalem to destroy the Temple because it was not being used for its proper purpose. Different cults were celebrating in the Temple. The LORD had no choice but to remove His house from the earth. How long will the LORD watch what is happening here? The best thing for people to do is to reverse the downward trend in morality that is taking over society. Ask yourself what you can do.

Psalm 107

New American Standard 1995	Hebrew
Psa. 107:1 Oh [a]give thanks to the LORD, for [b]He is good, For His lovingkindness is everlasting. 2 Let [a]the redeemed of the LORD say *so,* Whom He has [b]redeemed from the hand of the adversary 3 And [a]gathered from the lands, From the east and from the west, From the north and from the [1]south.	הֹדוּ לַיהוָה כִּי־טוֹב כִּי **Psa. 107:1** לְעוֹלָם חַסְדּוֹ : 2 יֹאמְרוּ גְּאוּלֵי יְהוָה אֲשֶׁר גְּאָלָם מִיַּד־צָר : 3 וּמֵאֲרָצוֹת קִבְּצָם מִמִּזְרָח וּמִמַּעֲרָב מִצָּפוֹן וּמִיָּם : 4 תָּעוּ בַמִּדְבָּר בִּישִׁימוֹן דָּרֶךְ עִיר מוֹשָׁב לֹא מָצָאוּ : 5 רְעֵבִים גַּם־צְמֵאִים נַפְשָׁם בָּהֶם תִּתְעַטָּף : 6 וַיִּצְעֲקוּ אֶל־יְהוָה בַּצַּר לָהֶם מִמְּצוּקוֹתֵיהֶם יַצִּילֵם : 7
Psa. 107:4 They [a]wandered in the wilderness in a [1]desert region; They did not find a way to [2]an inhabited [b]city. 5 *They were* hungry [1]and thirsty; Their [a]soul fainted within them. 6 Then they [a]cried out to the LORD in their trouble; He delivered them out of their distresses. 7 He led them also by a [1a]straight way, To go to [2b]an inhabited city. 8 [a]Let them give thanks to the LORD for His lovingkindness, And for His [1]wonders to the sons of men! 9 For He has [a]satisfied the [1]thirsty soul,	וַיַּדְרִיכֵם בְּדֶרֶךְ יְשָׁרָה לָלֶכֶת אֶל־ עִיר מוֹשָׁב : 8 יוֹדוּ לַיהוָה חַסְדּוֹ וְנִפְלְאוֹתָיו לִבְנֵי אָדָם : 9 כִּי־ הִשְׂבִּיעַ נֶפֶשׁ שֹׁקֵקָה וְנֶפֶשׁ רְעֵבָה מִלֵּא־טוֹב : 10 יֹשְׁבֵי חֹשֶׁךְ וְצַלְמָוֶת אֲסִירֵי עֳנִי וּבַרְזֶל : 11 כִּי־הִמְרוּ אִמְרֵי־אֵל וַעֲצַת עֶלְיוֹן נָאָצוּ : 12 וַיַּכְנַע בֶּעָמָל לִבָּם כָּשְׁלוּ וְאֵין עֹזֵר : 13 וַיִּזְעֲקוּ אֶל־יְהוָה בַּצַּר לָהֶם מִמְּצֻקוֹתֵיהֶם יוֹשִׁיעֵם : 14 יוֹצִיאֵם מֵחֹשֶׁךְ וְצַלְמָוֶת וּמוֹסְרוֹתֵיהֶם יְנַתֵּק : 15 יוֹדוּ לַיהוָה חַסְדּוֹ וְנִפְלְאוֹתָיו לִבְנֵי אָדָם : 16 כִּי־שִׁבַּר דַּלְתוֹת נְחֹשֶׁת וּבְרִיחֵי בַרְזֶל גִּדֵּעַ :

And the *b*hungry soul He has filled with what is good.

Psa. 107:10 There were those who *a*dwelt in darkness and in the shadow of death,

*b*Prisoners in [1]misery and [2]chains,

11 Because they had *a*rebelled against the words of God

And *b*spurned the *c*counsel of the Most High.

12 Therefore He humbled their heart with labor;

They stumbled and there was *a*none to help.

13 Then they *a*cried out to the LORD in their trouble;

He saved them out of their distresses.

14 He *b*brought them out of darkness and the shadow of death

And *b*broke their bands apart.

15 *a*Let them give thanks to the LORD for His lovingkindness,

And for His [1]wonders to the sons of men!

16 For He has *a*shattered gates of bronze

And cut bars of iron asunder.

Psa. 107:17 Fools, because of [1]their rebellious way,

And *a*because of their iniquities, were afflicted.

18 Their *a*soul abhorred all kinds of food,

And they *b*drew near to the *c*gates of death.

19 Then they cried out to the LORD in their trouble;

17 אֱוִלִים מִדֶּרֶךְ פִּשְׁעָם וּמֵעֲוֺנֹתֵיהֶם

יִתְעַנּוּ : 18 כָּל־אֹכֶל תְּתַעֵב נַפְשָׁם

וַיַּגִּיעוּ עַד־שַׁעֲרֵי מָוֶת : 19 וַיִּזְעֲקוּ

אֶל־יְהוָה בַּצַּר לָהֶם מִמְּצֻקוֹתֵיהֶם

יוֹשִׁיעֵם : 20 יִשְׁלַח דְּבָרוֹ וְיִרְפָּאֵם

וִימַלֵּט מִשְּׁחִיתוֹתָם : 21 יוֹדוּ

לַיהוָה חַסְדּוֹ וְנִפְלְאוֹתָיו לִבְנֵי

אָדָם : 22 וְיִזְבְּחוּ זִבְחֵי תוֹדָה

וִיסַפְּרוּ מַעֲשָׂיו בְּרִנָּה : 23 יוֹרְדֵי

הַיָּם בָּאֳנִיּוֹת עֹשֵׂי מְלָאכָה בְּמַיִם

רַבִּים : 24 הֵמָּה רָאוּ מַעֲשֵׂי יְהוָה

וְנִפְלְאוֹתָיו בִּמְצוּלָה : 25 וַיֹּאמֶר

וַיַּעֲמֵד רוּחַ סְעָרָה וַתְּרוֹמֵם גַּלָּיו : 26 יַעֲלוּ שָׁמַיִם יֵרְדוּ תְהוֹמוֹת נַפְשָׁם

בְּרָעָה תִתְמוֹגָג : 27 יָחוֹגּוּ וְיָנוּעוּ

28 כַּשִּׁכּוֹר וְכָל־חָכְמָתָם תִּתְבַּלָּע :

וַיִּצְעֲקוּ אֶל־יְהוָה בַּצַּר לָהֶם

וּמִמְּצוּקֹתֵיהֶם יוֹצִיאֵם : 29 יָקֵם

סְעָרָה לִדְמָמָה וַיֶּחֱשׁוּ גַּלֵּיהֶם : 30

וַיִּשְׂמְחוּ כִי־יִשְׁתֹּקוּ וַיַּנְחֵם אֶל־מְחוֹז

חֶפְצָם : 31 יוֹדוּ לַיהוָה חַסְדּוֹ

וְנִפְלְאוֹתָיו לִבְנֵי אָדָם : 32

וִירֹמְמוּהוּ בִּקְהַל־עָם וּבְמוֹשַׁב

זְקֵנִים יְהַלְלוּהוּ : 33 יָשֵׂם נְהָרוֹת

לְמִדְבָּר וּמֹצָאֵי מַיִם לְצִמָּאוֹן : 34

אֶרֶץ פְּרִי לִמְלֵחָה מֵרָעַת יֹשְׁבֵי

בָהּ : 35 יָשֵׂם מִדְבָּר לַאֲגַם־מַיִם

וְאֶרֶץ צִיָּה לְמֹצָאֵי מָיִם : 36 וַיּוֹשֶׁב

He saved them out of their distresses.
20 He *a*sent His word and *b*healed them,
And *c*delivered *them* from their ¹destructions.
21 *a*Let them give thanks to the LORD for His lovingkindness,
And for His ¹wonders to the sons of men!
22 Let them also offer *a*sacrifices of thanksgiving,
And *b*tell of His works with joyful singing.

Psa. 107:23 Those who *a*go down to the sea in ships,
Who do business on great waters;
24 They have seen the works of the LORD,
And His ¹wonders in the deep.
25 For He *a*spoke and raised up a *b*stormy wind,
Which ¹lifted up the waves ¹of the sea.
26 They rose up to the heavens, they went down to the depths;
Their soul *a*melted away in *their* misery.
27 They reeled and *a*staggered like a drunken man,
And ¹were at their wits' end.
28 Then they cried to the LORD in their trouble,
And He brought them out of their distresses.
29 He *a*caused the storm to be still,
So that the waves ¹of the sea were hushed.
30 Then they were glad because they were quiet,

שָׁם רְעֵבִים וַיְכוֹנְנוּ עִיר מוֹשָׁב ׃ 37 וַיִּזְרְעוּ שָׂדוֹת וַיִּטְּעוּ כְרָמִים וַיַּעֲשׂוּ פְּרִי תְבוּאָה ׃ 38 וַיְבָרֲכֵם וַיִּרְבּוּ מְאֹד וּבְהֶמְתָּם לֹא יַמְעִיט ׃ 39 וַיִּמְעֲטוּ וַיָּשֹׁחוּ מֵעֹצֶר רָעָה וְיָגוֹן ׃ 40 שֹׁפֵךְ בּוּז עַל־נְדִיבִים וַיַּתְעֵם בְּתֹהוּ לֹא־דָרֶךְ ׃ 41 וַיְשַׂגֵּב אֶבְיוֹן מֵעוֹנִי וַיָּשֶׂם כַּצֹּאן מִשְׁפָּחוֹת ׃ 42 יִרְאוּ יְשָׁרִים וְיִשְׂמָחוּ וְכָל־עַוְלָה קָפְצָה פִּיהָ ׃ 43 מִי־חָכָם וְיִשְׁמָר־אֵלֶּה וְיִתְבּוֹנְנוּ חַסְדֵי יְהוָה ׃

So He guided them to their desired haven.

31 *a*Let them give thanks to the LORD for His lovingkindness,

And for His [1b]wonders to the sons of men!

32 Let them *a*extol Him also *b*in the congregation of the people,

And *c*praise Him at the seat of the elders.

Psa. 107:33 He [1a]changes rivers into a [2]wilderness

And springs of water into a thirsty ground;

34 A *a*fruitful land into a *b*salt waste,

Because of the wickedness of those who dwell in it.

35 He [1a]changes a [2]wilderness into a pool of water

And a dry land into springs of water;

36 And there He makes the hungry to dwell,

So that they may establish [1a]an inhabited city,

37 And sow fields and *a*plant vineyards,

And [1]gather a fruitful harvest.

38 Also He blesses them and they *a*multiply greatly,

And He *b*does not let their cattle decrease.

Psa. 107:39 When they are *a*diminished and *b*bowed down

Through oppression, misery and sorrow,

40 He *a*pours contempt upon [1]princes

And *b*makes them wander *c*in a pathless waste.

<table>
<tr><td>

41   But He [a]sets the needy [1]securely on high away from affliction,

      And [b]makes *his* families like a flock.

42   The [a]upright see it and are glad;

      But all [b]unrighteousness shuts its mouth.

43   Who is [a]wise? Let him give heed to these things,

      And consider the [b]lovingkindnesses of the LORD.

</td><td></td></tr>
</table>

References

Psalm 107:1
[a]1 Chr 16:34; Ps 106:1; 118:1; 136:1; Jer 33:11
[b]2 Chr 5:13; 7:3; Ezra 3:11; Ps 100:5

Psalm 107:2
[a]Is 35:9, 10; 62:12; 63:4
[b]Ps 78:42; 106:10

Psalm 107:3
[1]Lit *sea*
[a]Deut 30:3; Neh 1:9; Ps 106:47; Is 11:12; 43:5; 56:8; Ezek 11:17; 20:34

Psalm 107:4
[1]Lit *waste*
[2]Or *a habitable city;* lit *a city of habitation*
[a]Num 14:33; 32:13; Deut 2:7; 32:10; Josh 5:6; 14:10
[b]Ps 107:7, 36

Psalm 107:5
[1]Lit *also*
[a]Ps 77:3

Psalm 107:6
[a]Ps 50:15; 107:13, 19, 28

Psalm 107:7
[1]Or *level*
[2]Or *a habitable city;* lit *a city of habitation*
[a]Ezra 8:21; Ps 5:8; Jer 31:9
[b]Ps 107:4, 36

Psalm 107:8
[1]I.e. wonderful acts
[a]Ps 107:15, 21, 31

Psalm 107:9
[1]Or *parched*
[a]Ps 22:26; 34:10; 63:5; 103:5
[b]Ps 146:7; Matt 5:6; Luke 1:53

Psalm 107:10
[1]Lit *affliction*
[2]Lit *irons*
[a]Ps 143:3; Is 42:7; Mic 7:8; Luke 1:79
[b]Job 36:8; Ps 102:20

Psalm 107:11
[a]Ps 78:40; 106:7; Lam 3:42
[b]Num 15:31; 2 Chr 36:16; Prov 1:25; Is 5:24
[c]Ps 73:24

Psalm 107:12
[a]Ps 22:11; 72:12

Psalm 107:13
[a]Ps 107:6

Psalm 107:14
[a]Ps 86:13; 107:10
[b]Ps 116:16; Jer 2:20; 30:8; Nah 1:13; Luke 13:16; Acts 12:7

Psalm 107:15
[1]I.e. wonderful acts
[a]Ps 107:8, 21, 31

Psalm 107:16
[a]Is 45:1, 2

Psalm 107:17
[1]Lit *the way of their transgression*
[a]Is 65:6, 7; Jer 30:14, 15; Lam 3:39; Ezek 24:23

Psalm 107:18
[a]Job 33:20; Ps 102:4
[b]Job 33:22; Ps 88:3
[c]Job 38:17; Ps 9:13

Psalm 107:20
[1]Or *pits*
[a]Ps 147:15, 18; Matt 8:8
[b]2 Kin 20:5; Ps 30:2; 103:3; 147:3
[c]Job 33:28, 30; Ps 30:3; 49:15; 56:13; 103:4

Psalm 107:21
[1]I.e. wonderful acts
[a]Ps 107:8, 15, 31

Psalm 107:22
[a]Lev 7:12; Ps 50:14; 116:17
[b]Ps 9:11; 73:28; 118:17

Psalm 107:23
[a]Is 42:10; Jon 1:3

Psalm 107:24
[1]I.e. wonderful acts

Psalm 107:25
[1]Lit *of it*
[a]Ps 105:31, 34
[b]Ps 148:8; Jon 1:4
[c]Ps 93:3, 4

Psalm 107:26
[a]Ps 22:14; 119:28

Psalm 107:27
[1]Lit *all their wisdom was swallowed up*
[a]Job 12:25; Is 24:20

Psalm 107:29
[1]Lit *of it*
[a]Ps 65:7; 89:9; Matt 8:26; Luke 8:24

Psalm 107:31
[1]I.e. wonderful acts
[a]Ps 107:8, 15, 21
[b]Ps 78:4; 111:4

Psalm 107:32
[a]Ps 34:3; 99:5; Is 25:1
[b]Ps 22:22, 25
[c]Ps 35:18

Psalm 107:33
[1]Or *turns*
[2]Or *desert*
[a]1 Kin 17:1, 7; Ps 74:15; Is 42:15; 50:2

Psalm 107:34
[a]Gen 13:10; 14:3; 19:24, 25; Deut 29:23
[b]Job 39:6; Jer 17:6

Psalm 107:35
[1]Or *turns*
[2]Or *desert*
[a]Ps 105:41; 114:8; Is 35:6, 7; 41:18

Psalm 107:36
[1]Or *a habitable city;* lit *a city of habitation*
[a]Ps 107:4, 7

Psalm 107:37
[1]Lit *acquire fruits of yield*
[a]2 Kin 19:29; Is 65:21; Amos 9:14

Psalm 107:38
[a]Gen 12:2; 17:20; Ex 1:7; Deut 1:10
[b]Deut 7:14

Psalm 107:39
[a]2 Kin 10:32; Ezek 5:11; 29:15
[b]Ps 38:6; 44:25; 57:6

Psalm 107:40
[1]Or *nobles*
[a]Job 12:21
[b]Job 12:24
[c]Deut 32:10

Psalm 107:41
[1]Lit *in an inaccessibly high place*
[a]1 Sam 2:8; Ps 59:1; 113:7, 8
[b]Job 21:11; Ps 78:52; 113:9

Psalm 107:42

[a]Job 22:19; Ps 52:6
[b]Job 5:16; Ps 63:11; Rom 3:19

Psalm 107:43
[a]Ps 64:9; Jer 9:12; Hos 14:9
[b]Ps 107:1

Targum

Psa. 107:1 Sing praise in the presence of the LORD, for he is good, for his goodness is forever. **2** The redeemed of the LORD will say [it], whom he redeemed from the hand of the oppressor. **3** And whom he gathered from the lands, from the east, and from the west, and from the north, and from the sea in the south. **4** Concerning the people of the house of Israel he prophesied and said, "The people of the house of Israel have wandered in the wilderness in a desolate path; they did not find an inhabited city." **5** Thirsty, yes, and hungry, their souls will grow weary. **6** And they prayed in the presence of the LORD went it went ill with them; he delivered them from their distress. **7** And he guided them on a straight way, to come to Jerusalem, the inhabited city. **8** Let them give thanks in the presence of the LORD because of his kindness, and tell his wonders to the sons of men. **9** For he has satisfied the soul of the empty, and filled with good things the soul of the hungry. **10** Concerning Zedekiah and the leaders of Israel he prophesied and said, "O Zedekiah and the leaders of Israel, who were exiled to Babylon and dwelt in darkness and the shadow of death, and became prisoners in the pain of iron fetters." **11** For they rebelled against the word of God, and rejected the counsel of the Most High. **12** And he broke their heart with toil; they stumbled, and there was none to help. **13** And they prayed in the presence of the LORD when it went ill with them; he redeemed them from their distress. **14** He brought them out of darkness and the shadow of death; and he will break their chains. **15** They will give thanks in the presence of the LORD because of his kindness, and tell his wonders to the sons of men. **16** For he shattered the doors of bronze, and cut down the bars of iron. **17** Concerning Hezekiah, king of the tribe of the house of Judah, he prophesied and said, "Hezekiah, king of the house of Judah, who refused to take a wife, was punished as the fools are punished because of their rebellious way and because of their iniquities." **18** Their soul will reject all food, and they arrive at the portals of death. **19** And they prayed in the presence of the LORD when it went ill with them, and he will redeem them from their distresses. **20** He will send the words of his healing and will heal them, and deliver [them] from being harmed. **21** They will give thanks in the presence of the LORD because of his kindness, and tell his wonders to the sons of men. **22** And they will sacrifice thanksgiving sacrifices, and will tell of his deeds in gladness. **23** Concerning the sailors of Jonah son of Amittai, he prophesied and said, "The sailors, those who go down to the sea in ships, those who do work on many waters – **24** They saw the deeds of the LORD, and his wonders in the deep." **25** And he gave command by his word, and raised up the storm and the gale, and its waves were lifted up high. **26** They go up towards heaven, they go down to the depths of the abysses; their souls will melt in misery. **27** They will tremble, they will totter like a man drunk with wine; and all their wisdom is destroyed. **28** And they prayed in the presence of the LORD when it went ill with them, and he will bring them out of their troubles. **29** He will make the wind cease to quietness, and their waves will be silent. **30** And they rejoiced, for they are silent; and he led them to the harbor they desired. **31** They will give thanks in the presence of the LORD because of his kindness, and tell his wonders to the sons of men. **32** And they exalt him in the assembly of the people, the house of Israel; and in the Sanhedrin of the wise they will praise him. **33** Concerning the generation of Joel son of Pethuel he prophesied and said: "When the house of Israel rebelled in the days of Joel the prophet, he brought a drought into the world; he made the rivers like the desert, and the sources of water like thirst." **34** The land of Israel that produces fruit became a waste like Sodom, which was overthrown because of the evil of its inhabitants. 35 When they returned to the Torah, he made the desert like a channel of water, and the parched land [became] sources of water. 36 And he made the hungry dwell there, and they set up an inhabited city. 37 And they sowed fields and planted vineyards, and they yielded fruit of produce. 38 And he blessed them and they multiplied greatly, and their livestock will not diminish. 39 And when they sinned, they diminished and became poor because of the affliction of misery and pain. 40 He pours contempt on the leaders, and made them wander in a void without a path. 41 But when they returned to the Torah, he exalted the needy from poverty, and made [them] like the flocks of the well-born families. 42 The upright will see and rejoice, but every liar's mouth is closed and sealed. 43 Would that the wise man keep these things, and discern the kindnesses of the LORD!

Spiritual Awareness

Introduction

This is the first Psalm of the fifth book of Psalms. It is a composition that expresses the thanks of those who were in places of danger but were rescued and arrived home safely. The sage Ibn Yachya related this Psalm to David's life. The Philistines had captured the Ark of the Covenant, and it was endangered. David returned the Ark to a haven of safety and sanctity. This is a hymn of thanksgiving.

Notes on this Psalm

The spiritual awareness of this Psalm is the understanding that it applied in David's day and today. The Sefirah Chesed sends the LORD's lovingkindness to humanity. The LORD asks people to live by the Laws in the Torah. If one is unsure how to accomplish this, just read any of the books of the prophets and the Gospels of Jesus of Nazareth. Jesus offered the best way through his own words and actions. When a person complies with the Torah, Chesed will flow with lovingkindness. This formula is the basics of the Sinai treaty, called the Ten Commandments.

The LORD said He can protect the people who want to be part of His kingdom. One becomes a member of the domain by following the Torah. The second part of the Sinai covenant (the Ten Commandments) is following the Law. It is a simple formula that Israel has struggled with for centuries. People struggle with this concept today. The primary central theme is the same whether your religion is Judaism or Christianity. Follow the Torah; the LORD will protect you, and Chesed will send His love.

Psalm 108

New American Standard 1995	Hebrew

Psa. 108:0 A Song, a Psalm of David.

Psa. 108:1 [a]My heart is steadfast, O God;

I will sing, I will sing praises, even with my [1]soul.

2 Awake, harp and lyre;

I will awaken the dawn!

3 I will give thanks to You, O LORD, among the peoples,

And I will sing praises to You among the nations.

4 For Your [a]lovingkindness is great [b]above the heavens,

And Your truth *reaches* to the skies.

5 [a]Be exalted, O God, above the heavens,

And Your glory above all the earth.

6 [a]That Your beloved may be delivered,

Save with Your right hand, and answer me!

Psa. 108:7 God has spoken in His [1]holiness:

"I will exult, I will portion out Shechem

And measure out the valley of Succoth.

8 "Gilead is Mine, Manasseh is Mine;

Ephraim also is the [1]helmet of My head;

[a]Judah is My [2]scepter.

9 "Moab is My washbowl;

Over Edom I shall throw My shoe;

שִׁיר מִזְמֹור לְדָוִד : **Psa. 108:1** נָכֹון

לִבִּי אֱלֹהִים אָשִׁירָה וַאֲזַמְּרָה אַף־

כְּבֹודִי : 3 עוּרָה הַנֵּבֶל וְכִנֹּור

אָעִירָה שָּׁחַר : 4 אֹודְךָ בָעַמִּים |

יְהוָה וַאֲזַמֶּרְךָ בַּל־אֻמִּים : 5 כִּי־

גָדֹול מֵעַל־שָׁמַיִם חַסְדֶּךָ וְעַד־

שְׁחָקִים אֲמִתֶּךָ : 6 רוּמָה עַל־שָׁמַיִם

אֱלֹהִים וְעַל כָּל־הָאָרֶץ כְּבֹודֶךָ : 7

לְמַעַן יֵחָלְצוּן יְדִידֶיךָ הֹושִׁיעָה

יְמִינְךָ וַעֲנֵנִי : 8 אֱלֹהִים | דִּבֶּר

בְּקָדְשֹׁו אֶעְלֹזָה אֲחַלְּקָה שְׁכֶם

וְעֵמֶק סֻכֹּות אֲמַדֵּד : 9 לִי גִלְעָד |

לִי מְנַשֶּׁה וְאֶפְרַיִם מָעֹוז רֹאשִׁי

יְהוּדָה מְחֹקְקִי : 10 מֹואָב | סִיר

רַחְצִי עַל־אֱדֹום אַשְׁלִיךְ נַעֲלִי

עֲלֵי־פְלֶשֶׁת אֶתְרֹועָע : 11 מִי יֹבִלֵנִי

עִיר מִבְצָר מִי נָחַנִי עַד־אֱדֹום : 12

הֲלֹא־אֱלֹהִים זְנַחְתָּנוּ וְלֹא־תֵצֵא

אֱלֹהִים בְּצִבְאֹתֵינוּ : 13 הָבָה־לָּנוּ

עֶזְרָת מִצָּר וְשָׁוְא תְּשׁוּעַת אָדָם : 14

בֵּאלֹהִים נַעֲשֶׂה־חָיִל וְהוּא יָבוּס

צָרֵינוּ :

Over Philistia I will shout aloud."

Psa. 108:10   *ª*Who will bring me into the besieged city?

Who [1]will lead me to Edom?

[11]   Have not You Yourself, O God, *ª*rejected us?

And will You not go forth with our armies, O God?

[12]   Oh give us help against the adversary,

For *ª*deliverance [1]by man is in vain.

[13]   [1]Through God we will do valiantly,

And *ª*it is He who shall tread down our adversaries.

References

Psalm 108:1
[1]Lit *glory*
[a]Ps 57:7-11; 108:1-5

Psalm 108:4
[a]Num 14:18; Deut 7:9; Ps 36:5; 100:5; Mic 7:18-20
[b]Ps 113:4

Psalm 108:5
[a]Ps 57:5

Psalm 108:6
[a]Ps 60:5-12; 108:6-13

Psalm 108:7
[1]Or *sanctuary*

Psalm 108:8
[1]Lit *protection*
[2]Or *lawgiver*
[a]Gen 49:10

Psalm 108:10
[1]Or *has led*
[a]Ps 60:9

Psalm 108:11
[a]Ps 44:9

Psalm 108:12
[1]Lit *of*
[a]Is 30:3

Psalm 108:13
[1]Or *In* or *With*
[a]Is 60:12; 63:1-4

Targum

Psa. 108:1 A song and Psalm composed by David. ² My heart is firm, O God; I will praise and sing indeed, my glory. ³ Sing praise, O harp and lyre; I will sing praise at dawn. ⁴ I will give thanks in your presence among the peoples, O LORD, and I will sing praise to you among the nations. ⁵ For your goodness is great above the heavens, and your truth reaches to the sky. ⁶ Be exalted above the heavens, O God, and may your glory be on all the inhabitants of the earth. ⁷ So that your beloved ones will be delivered; redeem with your right hand and answer me. ⁸ God speaks from the place of his presence ; I will be glad, I will divide spoil with the inhabitants of Shechem; and with the inhabitants of the plain of Succoth I will measure the border. ⁹ Mine is Gilead, mine is Manasseh; those of the house of Ephraim are the strength of my head, and my scribe is from those of the house of Judah. ¹⁰ I have trampled the Moabites like my washing-pot; I will cast my sandal over the kingdom of Edom; I will shout over the kingdom of the Philistines. ¹¹ And now because I sinned, who will lead me to the fortress of wicked Rome? Who led me to Constantinople of Edom? ¹² Behold, because we have sinned in the presence of the LORD he has forsaken us, and his presence does not go out with our armies. ¹³ Give us help from the oppressor, for vain is the redemption of the son of man. ¹⁴ In God we shall show might, and he will trample our oppressors.

Spiritual Awareness

Introduction

This Psalm is an almost exact duplication of Psalms 57 and 60. The Psalm says that the Messiah will deliver the people from Exile, and she will triumph over all of her enemies.

Notes on the Psalm

Refer to the notes in Psalms 57 and 60.

Psalm 109

New American Standard 1995	Hebrew
Psa. 109:0 For the choir director. A Psalm of David. **Psa. 109:1** O *God of my praise, *Do not be silent! 2 For they have opened the [1]wicked and *deceitful mouth against me; They have spoken [2]against me with a *lying tongue. 3 They have also surrounded me with words of hatred, And fought against me *without cause. 4 In return *for my love they act as my accusers; But *I am *in* prayer. 5 Thus they have [1a]repaid me evil for good And *hatred for my love. **Psa. 109:6** Appoint a wicked man over him, And let an [1a]accuser stand at his right hand. 7 When he is judged, let him *come forth guilty, And let his *prayer become sin. 8 Let *his days be few; Let *another take his office. 9 Let his *children be fatherless And his *wife a widow. 10 Let his *children wander about and beg;	לַמְנַצֵּחַ לְדָוִד מִזְמוֹר **Psa. 109:1** אֱלֹהֵי תְהִלָּתִי אַל־תֶּחֱרַשׁ: 2 כִּי פִי רָשָׁע וּפִי־מִרְמָה עָלַי פָּתָחוּ דִּבְּרוּ אִתִּי לְשׁוֹן שָׁקֶר: 3 וְדִבְרֵי שִׂנְאָה סְבָבוּנִי וַיִּלָּחֲמוּנִי חִנָּם: 4 תַּחַת־ אַהֲבָתִי יִשְׂטְנוּנִי וַאֲנִי תְפִלָּה: 5 וַיָּשִׂימוּ עָלַי רָעָה תַּחַת טוֹבָה וְשִׂנְאָה תַּחַת אַהֲבָתִי: 6 הַפְקֵד עָלָיו רָשָׁע וְשָׂטָן יַעֲמֹד עַל־יְמִינוֹ: 7 בְּהִשָּׁפְטוֹ יֵצֵא רָשָׁע וּתְפִלָּתוֹ תִּהְיֶה לַחֲטָאָה: 8 יִהְיוּ־יָמָיו מְעַטִּים פְּקֻדָּתוֹ יִקַּח אַחֵר: 9 יִהְיוּ־ בָנָיו יְתוֹמִים וְאִשְׁתּוֹ אַלְמָנָה: 10 וְנוֹעַ יָנוּעוּ בָנָיו וְשִׁאֵלוּ וְדָרְשׁוּ מֵחָרְבוֹתֵיהֶם: 11 יְנַקֵּשׁ נוֹשֶׁה לְכָל־ אֲשֶׁר־לוֹ וְיָבֹזּוּ זָרִים יְגִיעוֹ: 12 אַל־ יְהִי־לוֹ מֹשֵׁךְ חָסֶד וְאַל־יְהִי חוֹנֵן לִיתוֹמָיו: 13 יְהִי־אַחֲרִיתוֹ לְהַכְרִית בְּדוֹר אַחֵר יִמַּח שְׁמָם: 14 יִזָּכֵר ׀ עֲוֹן אֲבֹתָיו אֶל־יְהוָה וְחַטַּאת אִמּוֹ אַל־תִּמָּח: 15 יִהְיוּ נֶגֶד־יְהוָה תָּמִיד וְיַכְרֵת מֵאֶרֶץ זִכְרָם: 16 יַעַן אֲשֶׁר ׀ לֹא זָכַר עֲשׂוֹת חָסֶד וַיִּרְדֹּף אִישׁ־

And let them [b]seek *sustenance* [1]far from their ruined homes.

11 Let [a]the creditor [1]seize all that he has,

And let [b]strangers plunder the product of his labor.

12 Let there be none to [1a]extend lovingkindness to him,

Nor [b]any to be gracious to his fatherless children.

13 Let his [a]posterity be [1]cut off;

In a following generation let their [b]name be blotted out.

Psa. 109:14 Let [a]the iniquity of his fathers be remembered [1]before the LORD,

And do not let the sin of his mother be [b]blotted out.

15 Let [a]them be before the LORD continually,

That He may [b]cut off their memory from the earth;

16 Because he did not remember to show lovingkindness,

But persecuted the [a]afflicted and needy man,

And the [b]despondent in heart, to [c]put *them* to death.

17 He also loved cursing, so [a]it came to him;

And he did not delight in blessing, so it was far from him.

18 But he [a]clothed himself with cursing as with his garment,

And it [b]entered into [1]his body like water

And like oil into his bones.

19 Let it be to him as [a]a garment with which he covers himself,

עָנִי וְאֶבְיוֹן וְנִכְאֵה לֵבָב לְמוֹתֵת : 17

וַיֶּאֱהַב קְלָלָה וַתְּבוֹאֵהוּ וְלֹא־חָפֵץ בִּבְרָכָה וַתִּרְחַק מִמֶּנּוּ : 18 וַיִּלְבַּשׁ קְלָלָה כְּמַדּוֹ וַתָּבֹא כַמַּיִם בְּקִרְבּוֹ וְכַשֶּׁמֶן בְּעַצְמוֹתָיו : 19 תְּהִי־לוֹ כְּבֶגֶד יַעְטֶה וּלְמֵזַח תָּמִיד יַחְגְּרֶהָ : זֹאת פְּעֻלַּת שֹׂטְנַי מֵאֵת יְהוָה 20 וְהַדֹּבְרִים רָע עַל־נַפְשִׁי : 21 וְאַתָּה יְהוִה אֲדֹנָי עֲשֵׂה־אִתִּי לְמַעַן שְׁמֶךָ כִּי־טוֹב חַסְדְּךָ הַצִּילֵנִי : 22 כִּי־עָנִי וְאֶבְיוֹן אָנֹכִי וְלִבִּי חָלַל בְּקִרְבִּי : 23 כְּצֵל־כִּנְטוֹתוֹ נֶהֱלָכְתִּי נִנְעַרְתִּי כָּאַרְבֶּה : 24 בִּרְכַּי כָּשְׁלוּ מִצּוֹם וּבְשָׂרִי כָּחַשׁ מִשָּׁמֶן : 25 וַאֲנִי הָיִיתִי חֶרְפָּה לָהֶם יִרְאוּנִי יְנִיעוּן רֹאשָׁם : 26 עָזְרֵנִי יְהוָה אֱלֹהָי הוֹשִׁיעֵנִי כְחַסְדֶּךָ : 27 וְיֵדְעוּ כִּי־יָדְךָ זֹּאת אַתָּה יְהוָה עֲשִׂיתָהּ : 28 יְקַלְלוּ־הֵמָּה וְאַתָּה תְבָרֵךְ קָמוּ וַיֵּבֹשׁוּ וְעַבְדְּךָ יִשְׂמָח : 29 יִלְבְּשׁוּ שׂוֹטְנַי כְּלִמָּה וְיַעֲטוּ כַמְעִיל בָּשְׁתָּם : 30 אוֹדֶה יְהוָה מְאֹד בְּפִי וּבְתוֹךְ רַבִּים אֲהַלְלֶנּוּ : 31 כִּי־יַעֲמֹד לִימִין אֶבְיוֹן לְהוֹשִׁיעַ מִשֹּׁפְטֵי נַפְשׁוֹ :

And for a belt with which he constantly *b*girds himself.

20   [1]Let this be the *a*reward of my accusers from the LORD,

And of those who *b*speak evil against my soul.

Psa. 109:21   But You, O [1]GOD, the Lord, deal *kindly* with me *a*for Your name's sake;

Because *b*Your lovingkindness is good, deliver me;

22   For *a*I am afflicted and needy,

And [1]my heart is *b*wounded within me.

23   I am passing *a*like a shadow when it lengthens;

I am shaken off *b*like the locust.

24   My *a*knees [1]are weak from *b*fasting,

And my flesh has grown lean, without fatness.

25   I also have become a *a*reproach to them;

When they see me, they *b*wag their head.

Psa. 109:26   *a*Help me, O LORD my God;

Save me according to Your lovingkindness.

27   [1]And let them *a*know that this is Your hand;

You, LORD, have done it.

28   *a*Let them curse, but You bless;

When they arise, they shall be ashamed,

But Your *b*servant shall be glad.

29   [1]Let *a*my accusers be clothed with dishonor,

And [2]let them *b*cover themselves with their own shame as with a robe.

Psa. 109:30   With my mouth I will give thanks abundantly to the LORD;

And in the midst of many *ᵃ*I will praise Him.

31   For He stands *ᵃ*at the right hand of the needy,

To save him from those who *ᵇ*judge his soul.

References

Psalm 109:1
[a]Deut 10:21
[b]Ps 28:1; 83:1

Psalm 109:2
[1]Lit *wicked mouth and the deceitful*
[2]Lit *with*
[a]Ps 10:7; 52:4
[b]Ps 120:2

Psalm 109:3
[a]Ps 35:7; 69:4; John 15:25

Psalm 109:4
[a]Ps 38:20
[b]Ps 69:13; 141:5

Psalm 109:5
[1]Lit *laid upon me*
[a]Ps 35:12; 38:20
[b]John 7:7; 10:32

Psalm 109:6
[1]Or *adversary, Satan*
[a]Zech 3:1

Psalm 109:7
[a]Ps 1:5
[b]Prov 28:9

Psalm 109:8
[a]Ps 55:23
[b]Acts 1:20

Psalm 109:9
[a]Ex 22:24
[b]Jer 18:21

Psalm 109:10
[1]Or *out of their desolate places*
[a]Gen 4:12; Job 30:5-8; Ps 59:15
[b]Ps 37:25

Psalm 109:11
[1]Lit *ensnare, strike at*
[a]Neh 5:7; Job 5:5; 20:15
[b]Is 1:7; Lam 5:2; Ezek 7:21

Psalm 109:12
[1]Lit *continue*
[a]Ezra 7:28; 9:9
[b]Job 5:4; Is 9:17

Psalm 109:13
[1]Lit *for cutting off*
[a]Job 18:19; Ps 21:10; 37:28
[b]Ps 9:5; Prov 10:7

Psalm 109:14
[1]Lit *to*
[a]Ex 20:5; Num 14:18; Is 65:6, 7; Jer 32:18
[b]Neh 4:5; Jer 18:23

Psalm 109:15
[a]Ps 90:8; Jer 16:17
[b]Job 18:17; Ps 34:16

Psalm 109:16
[a]Ps 37:14
[b]Ps 34:18
[c]Ps 37:32; 94:6

Psalm 109:17
[a]Prov 14:14; Ezek 35:9; Matt 7:2

Psalm 109:18
[1]Lit *his inward parts*
[a]Ps 73:6; 109:29; Ezek 7:27

*b*Num 5:22

Psalm 109:19
*a*Ps 73:6; 109:29; Ezek 7:27
*b*2 Sam 22:40; Ps 30:11; Is 11:5

Psalm 109:20
[1]Lit *This is*
*a*Ps 54:5; 94:23; Is 3:11; 2 Tim 4:14
*b*Ps 41:5; 71:10

Psalm 109:21
[1]Heb *YHWH,* usually rendered *LORD*
*a*Ps 23:3; 25:11; 79:9; 106:8; Ezek 36:22
*b*Ps 69:16

Psalm 109:22
[1]Lit *one has pierced my heart within me*
*a*Ps 40:17; 86:1
*b*Job 24:12; Ps 143:4; Prov 18:14

Psalm 109:23
*a*Ps 102:11
*b*Ex 10:19; Job 39:20

Psalm 109:24
[1]Or *totter*
*a*Heb 12:12
*b*Ps 35:13

Psalm 109:25
*a*Ps 22:6
*b*Ps 22:7; Jer 18:16; Lam 2:15; Matt 27:39; Mark 15:29

Psalm 109:26
*a*Ps 119:86

Psalm 109:27
[1]Or *That they may know*
*a*Job 37:7

Psalm 109:28
[a]2 Sam 16:11, 12
[b]Is 65:14

Psalm 109:29
[1]Or *My accusers will be*
[2]Or *they will cover*
[a]Job 8:22; Ps 132:18
[b]Job 8:22; Ps 35:26

Psalm 109:30
[a]Ps 22:22; 35:18; 111:1

Psalm 109:31
[a]Ps 16:8; 73:23; 110:5; 121:5
[b]Ps 37:33

Targum

Psa. 109:1 For praise, composed by David; a psalm. O God, my praise, do not be silent. [2] For the mouth of wickedness and the mouth of deceit are open against me, they have spoken with me [with] a lying tongue. [3] And those who speak hatred have surrounded me, and fought against me for no cause. [4] Because I have loved, they opposed me; but I will pray. [5] And they gave me evil for good, and hatred where I had given love. [6] Appoint over him a wicked man, and may an adversary stand at his right hand. [7] When he is judged, let him come out a sinner, and may his prayer become an act of sin. [8] May his days be few, may [another inherit the number of his years.] [9] May his sons be orphans, and his wife a widow. [10] And may his sons yet wander, and beg, and seek what has become their wasteland. [11] May the creditor gather up all that is his, and may strangers plunder his toil. [12] May he have none to extend kindness, and may he have none to pity his orphans. [13] May his end be destruction; may their name be effaced in the next generation. [14] May the iniquity of his fathers be remembered in the presence of the LORD; and may his mother's guilt not be effaced. [15] May they be facing the decree of the LORD always; and may their memory perish from the earth. [16] Because he did not remember to do good, and persecutes the poor and needy man, and the lowly of heart, to be slain. [17] And he loves cursing, and it came to him; and he took no pleasure in blessing, and it was far from him. [18] And he wore cursing like a garment, and it entered his body like water, and was like oil to his limbs. [19] May it be to him like a garment, let him be wrapped in it; may he gird himself with it as a perpetual belt. [20] This is the deed of those who oppose me from [following] the LORD, and of those who speak evil to my soul. [21] And you, O God, the LORD, deal with me for your name's sake; deliver me according to your goodness and kindness. [22] For I am poor and needy, and my heart is quiet within me. [23] I am finished, like a shadow when it lengthens; I have wandered like a locust. [24] My knees stumble from fasting; my flesh is lean, and no longer fat. [25] And I have become a disgrace to them; they will see me, they will shake their heads. [26] Help me, O LORD, my God; redeem me according to your kindness. [27] And they will know that this plague, you, O LORD, have done it. [28] They will curse, but you will bless; they will arise and be disappointed, but your servant will rejoice. [29] Those who oppose me will be clothed in shame, and their infamy will cover them like a cloak. [30] I will thank the LORD greatly with my mouth, and I will praise him in the midst of the sages. [31] For he will stand at the right hand of the needy, to redeem from the discords of his soul.

Spiritual Awareness

Introduction

David wrote this Psalm as he fled from the wrath of King Saul. People had been slandering David to Saul. The Midrash Shocher Tov says these words describe God's unique relationship. The work is concluded with confidence that God will respond when called.

Superscript

To the Sefirah Netzach who grants victory, by David a psalm. O God of my praise, do not keep silent.

Verse twenty

David calls out to the Sefirah Chesed for the LORD's lovingkindness.

But You, O God, my Master, Who are merciful even in judgment, deal with me for Your Name's sake; when the Sefirah Chesed sends Your lovingkindness is gracious again, deliver me.

Verse twenty-five

Help me, O LORD God, save me by the lovingkindness of the Sefirah Chesed.

Psalm 110

New American Standard 1995

Psa. 110:0 A Psalm of David.

Psa. 110:1 [a]The LORD says to my Lord:
"[b]Sit at My right hand
Until I make [c]Your enemies a footstool for Your feet."
2 The LORD will stretch forth Your strong [a]scepter from Zion, *saying,*
"[b]Rule in the midst of Your enemies."
3 Your [a]people [1]will volunteer freely in the day of Your [2]power;
[b]In [3]holy array, from the womb of the dawn,
[4]Your youth are to You *as* the [c]dew.

Psa. 110:4 [a]The LORD has sworn and will [b]not [1]change His mind,
"You are a [c]priest forever
According to the order of Melchizedek."
5 The Lord is [a]at Your right hand;
He [1]will [b]shatter kings in the [c]day of His wrath.
6 He will [a]judge among the nations,
He [1]will fill *them* with [b]corpses,
He [2]will [c]shatter the [3]chief men over a broad country.
7 He will [a]drink from the brook by the wayside;
Therefore He will [b]lift up *His* head.

Hebrew

Psa. 110:1 לְדָוִ֗ד מִ֫זְמ֥וֹר נְאֻ֤ם יְהוָ֨ה ׀
לַֽאדֹנִ֗י שֵׁ֥ב לִֽימִינִ֑י עַד־אָשִׁ֥ית
אֹ֝יְבֶ֗יךָ הֲדֹ֣ם לְרַגְלֶֽיךָ׃ 2 מַטֵּֽה־עֻזְּךָ֗
יִשְׁלַ֣ח יְ֭הוָה מִצִּיּ֑וֹן רְ֝דֵ֗ה בְּקֶ֣רֶב
אֹיְבֶֽיךָ׃ 3 עַמְּךָ֣ נְדָבֹת֮ בְּי֪וֹם חֵ֫ילֶ֥ךָ
בְּהַדְרֵי־קֹ֭דֶשׁ מֵרֶ֣חֶם מִשְׁחָ֑ר לְ֝ךָ֗ טַ֣ל
יַלְדֻתֶֽיךָ׃ 4 נִשְׁבַּ֤ע יְהוָ֨ה ׀ וְלֹ֬א יִנָּחֵ֗ם
אַתָּֽה־כֹהֵ֥ן לְעוֹלָ֑ם עַל־דִּ֝בְרָתִ֗י
מַלְכִּי־צֶֽדֶק׃ 5 אֲדֹנָ֥י עַל־יְמִֽינְךָ֑
מָחַ֖ץ בְּיוֹם־אַפּ֣וֹ מְלָכִֽים׃ 6 יָדִ֣ין
בַּ֭גּוֹיִם מָלֵ֣א גְוִיּ֑וֹת מָ֥חַץ רֹ֝֗אשׁ עַל־
אֶ֥רֶץ רַבָּֽה׃ 7 מִ֭נַּחַל בַּדֶּ֣רֶךְ יִשְׁתֶּ֑ה
עַל־כֵּ֝֗ן יָרִ֥ים רֹֽאשׁ׃

References

Psalm 110:1
[a]Matt 22:44; Mark 12:36; Luke 20:42, 43; Acts 2:34, 35; Heb 1:13
[b]Matt 26:64; Eph 1:20; Col 3:1; Heb 1:3; 8:1; 10:12; 12:2
[c]1 Cor 15:25; Eph 1:22

Psalm 110:2
[a]Ps 45:6; Jer 48:17; Ezek 19:14
[b]Ps 2:9; 72:8; Dan 7:13, 14

Psalm 110:3
[1]Lit *will be freewill offerings*
[2]Or *army*
[3]Or *the splendor of holiness*
[4]Or *The dew of Your youth is Yours*
[a]Judg 5:2; Neh 11:2
[b]1 Chr 16:29; Ps 96:9
[c]2 Sam 17:12; Mic 5:7

Psalm 110:4
[1]Lit *be sorry*
[a]Heb 7:21
[b]Num 23:19
[c]Zech 6:13; Heb 5:6, 10; 6:20; 7:17, 21

Psalm 110:5
[1]Or *has shattered*
[a]Ps 16:8; 109:31
[b]Ps 68:14; 76:12
[c]Ps 2:5, 12; Rom 2:5; Rev 6:17

Psalm 110:6
[1]Or *has filled*
[2]Or *has shattered*
[3]Lit *head over*
[a]Is 2:4; Joel 3:12; Mic 4:3
[b]Is 66:24
[c]Ps 68:21

Targum

Psa. 110:1 Composed by David, a psalm. The LORD said in his decree to make me lord of all Israel, but he said to me, "Wait still for Saul of the tribe of Benjamin to die, for one reign must not encroach on [another; and afterwards I will make your enemies a prop for your feet." ANOTHER TARGUM: The LORD spoke by his decree to give me the dominion in exchange for sitting in study of Torah. "Wait at my right hand until I make your enemies a prop for your feet." ANOTHER TARGUM: The LORD said in his decree to appoint me ruler over Israel, but the LORD said to me, "Wait for Saul of the tribe of Benjamin to pass away from the world; and afterwards you will inherit the kingship, and I will make your enemies a prop for your feet."] [2] The LORD will send from Zion the rod of your strength, and you will rule in the midst of your enemies. [3] Your people are those of the house of Israel who devote themselves to the Torah; you will be helped in the day of your making battle with them; in the glories of holiness the mercies of God will hasten to you like the descent of dew; your offspring dwell securely. [4] The LORD has sworn and will not turn aside, that you are appointed leader in the age to come, because of the merit that you were a righteous king. [5] The presence of the LORD is at your right hand; he struck down kings on the day of his anger. [6] He was appointed judge over the Gentiles; the earth is full of the bodies of the slain wicked; he smote the heads of kings on the earth, very many. [7] He will receive instruction from the mouth of the prophet on the way; because of this, he will lift up his head.

Spiritual Awareness

Introduction

Midrash Shocher Tov has an interesting interpretation of the Psalm. It is presented as a hymn of gratitude from the LORD to Abraham. The LORD calls Abraham "my master." The Midrash explains that the nations of the world were asleep, preventing them from recognizing the LORD. It was Abraham who woke them up to the LORD's presence. If this did not happen, the Creation would have amounted to nothing. The LORD created the universe so the people could know of His presence. The knowledge and presence of the LORD through the Sefirot are a gift to humanity. What good is a gift of this nature if it is never recognized?

Verse one

לְדָוִד (l'david) – means "to David." The NASB translated this verse as "A psalm of David." Hirsch translates it as "to David, a psalm." This verse is incorrectly translated in Christian Bibles because the church uses this verse to exemplify Jesus Christ as the Messiah who sits on the right hand of the LORD God. The Psalm was written to David and not by David. Therefore, the correct translation is:

To David. A Psalm. The LORD said to my master: Wait at My right hand, until I make your enemies your footstool.

לַאדֹנִי (ladonee) – means "my master." In this verse, the master is a reference to King David. It was common for a person working in the royal court to address the King in this manner.

APPENDIX

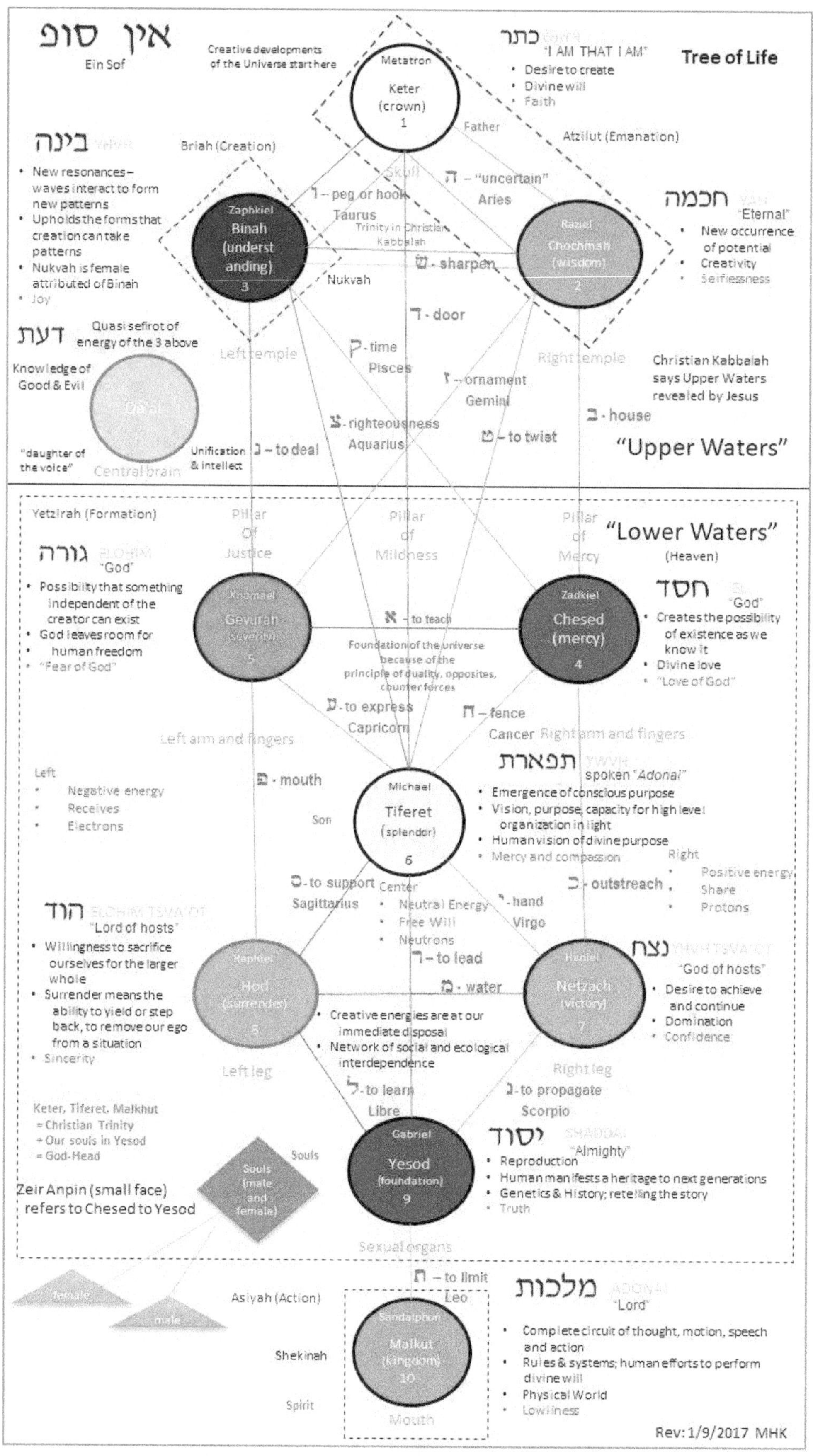

אין סוף
Ein Sof
Tree of Life
Creative developments of the Universe start here
כתר
"I AM THAT I AM"
• Desire to create
• Divine will
• Faith
Metatron
Keter (crown)
1
Father
Briah (Creation)
Atzilut (Emanation)
בינה
• New resonances – waves interact to form new patterns
• Upholds the forms that creation can take patterns
• Nukvah is female attributed of Binah
• Joy
Zaphkiel
Binah (understanding)
3
ה – "uncertain"
Aries
ו – peg or hook
Taurus
Trinity in Christian Kabbalah
Nukvah
ש – sharpen
חכמה
"Eternal"
• New occurrence of potential
• Creativity
• Selflessness
Raziel
Chochmah (wisdom)
2
ד – door
דעת
Quasi sefirot of energy of the 3 above
Knowledge of Good & Evil
Da'at
"daughter of the voice"
פ – time
Pisces
ז – ornament
Gemini
ב – house
Christian Kabbalah says Upper Waters revealed by Jesus
"Upper Waters"
צ – righteousness
Aquarius
נ – to deal
כ – to twist
Left temple
Central brain
Right temple
Unification & intellect
Yetzirah (Formation)
Pillar Of Justice
Pillar of Mildness
Pillar of Mercy
"Lower Waters"
(Heaven)
גורה
"God"
• Possibility that something independent of the creator can exist
• God leaves room for human freedom
• "Fear of God"
Khamael
Gevurah (severity)
5
א – to teach
Foundation of the universe because of the principle of duality, opposites, counter forces
חסד
"God"
• Creates the possibility of existence as we know it
• Divine love
• "Love of God"
Zadkiel
Chesed (mercy)
4
ע – to express
Capricorn
ח – fence
Cancer
Left arm and fingers
Right arm and fingers
Left
• Negative energy
• Receives
• Electrons
פ – mouth
Michael
Tiferet (splendor)
6
Son
תפארת
spoken "Adonai"
• Emergence of conscious purpose
• Vision, purpose, capacity for high level organization in light
• Human vision of divine purpose
• Mercy and compassion
Right
• Positive energy
• Share
• Protons
ס – to support
Center
Sagittarius
• Neutral Energy
• Free Will
• Neutrons
י – hand
Virgo
ב – outstreach
הוד
"Lord of hosts"
• Willingness to sacrifice ourselves for the larger whole
• Surrender means the ability to yield or step back, to remove our ego from a situation
• Sincerity
Raphiel
Hod (Surrender)
8
ר – to lead
מ – water
Creative energies are at our immediate disposal
Network of social and ecological interdependence
נצח
"God of hosts"
• Desire to achieve and continue
• Domination
• Confidence
Haniel
Netzach (victory)
7
Left leg
Right leg
ל – to learn
Libre
נ – to propagate
Scorpio
Keter, Tiferet, Malkhut
= Christian Trinity
+ Our souls in Yesod
= God-Head
Zeir Anpin (small face) refers to Chesed to Yesod
Souls (male and female)
Souls
Gabriel
Yesod (foundation)
9
יסוד
"Almighty"
• Reproduction
• Human manifests a heritage to next generations
• Genetics & History; retelling the story
• Truth
Sexual organs
female
male
ת – to limit
Leo
Asiyah (Action)
Shekinah
Spirit
Sandalphon
Malkut (kingdom)
10
Mouth
מלכות
"Lord"
• Complete circuit of thought, motion, speech and action
• Rules & systems; human efforts to perform divine will
• Physical World
• Lowliness
Rev: 1/9/2017 MHK

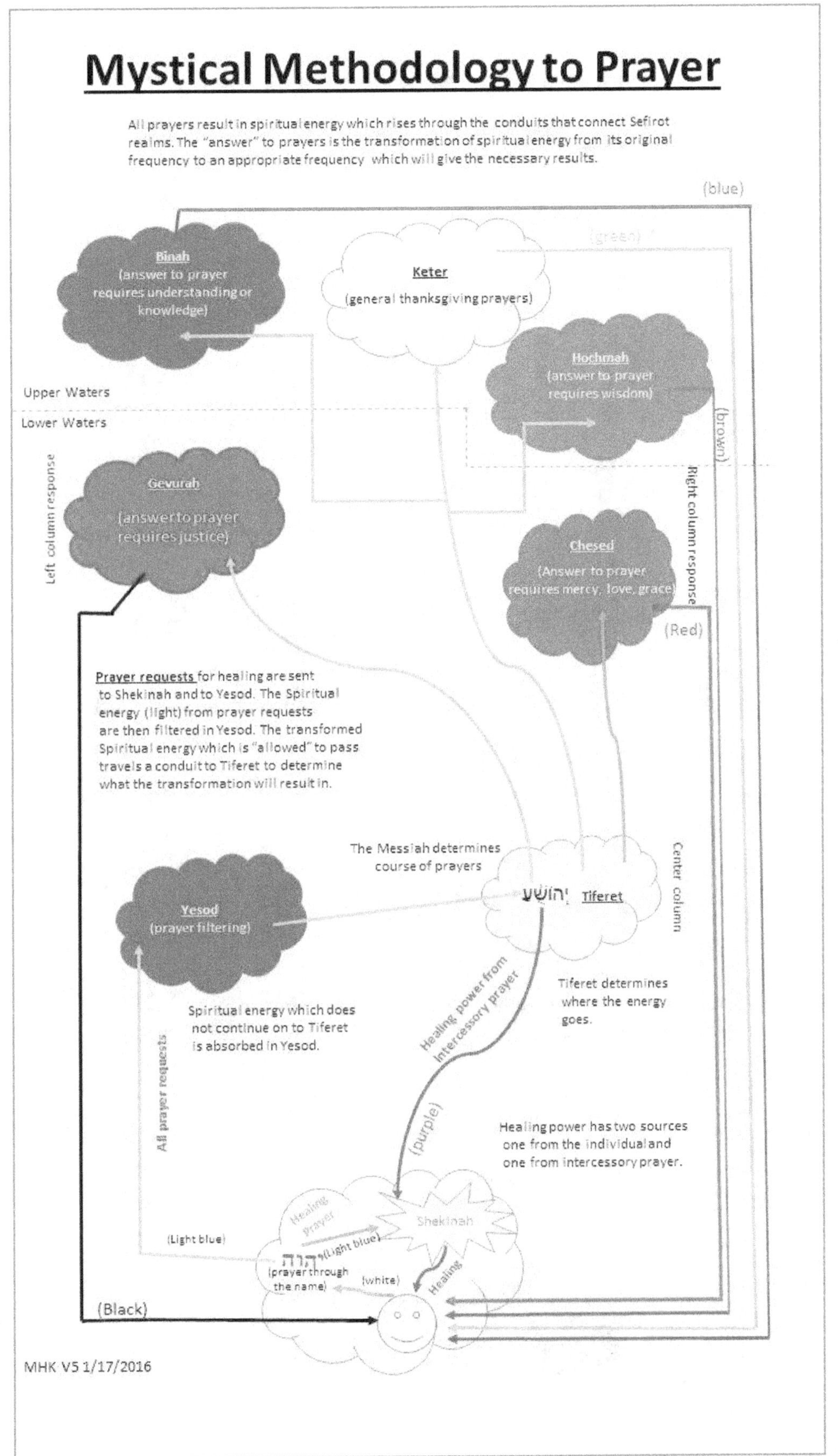

Mystical Methodology to Prayer
All prayers result in spiritual energy which rises through the conduits that connect Sefirot realms. The "answer" to prayers is the transformation of spiritual energy from its original frequency to an appropriate frequency which will give the necessary results.
(blue)
(green)
Binah (answer to prayer requires understanding or knowledge)
Keter (general thanksgiving prayers)
Hochmah (answer to prayer requires wisdom)
(brown)
Upper Waters
Lower Waters
Left column response
Gevurah (answer to prayer requires justice)
Chesed (Answer to prayer requires mercy, love, grace)
Right column response
(Red)
Prayer requests for healing are sent to Shekinah and to Yesod. The Spiritual energy (light) from prayer requests are then filtered in Yesod. The transformed Spiritual energy which is "allowed" to pass travels a conduit to Tiferet to determine what the transformation will result in.
The Messiah determines course of prayers
יהושע Tiferet
Center column
Yesod (prayer filtering)
Spiritual energy which does not continue on to Tiferet is absorbed in Yesod.
All prayer requests
Healing power from intercessory prayer
Tiferet determines where the energy goes.
(purple)
Healing power has two sources one from the individual and one from intercessory prayer.
Healing prayer
Shekinah
(Light blue)
(Light blue)
יהוה (prayer through the name)
(white)
Healing
(Black)
MHK V5 1/17/2016

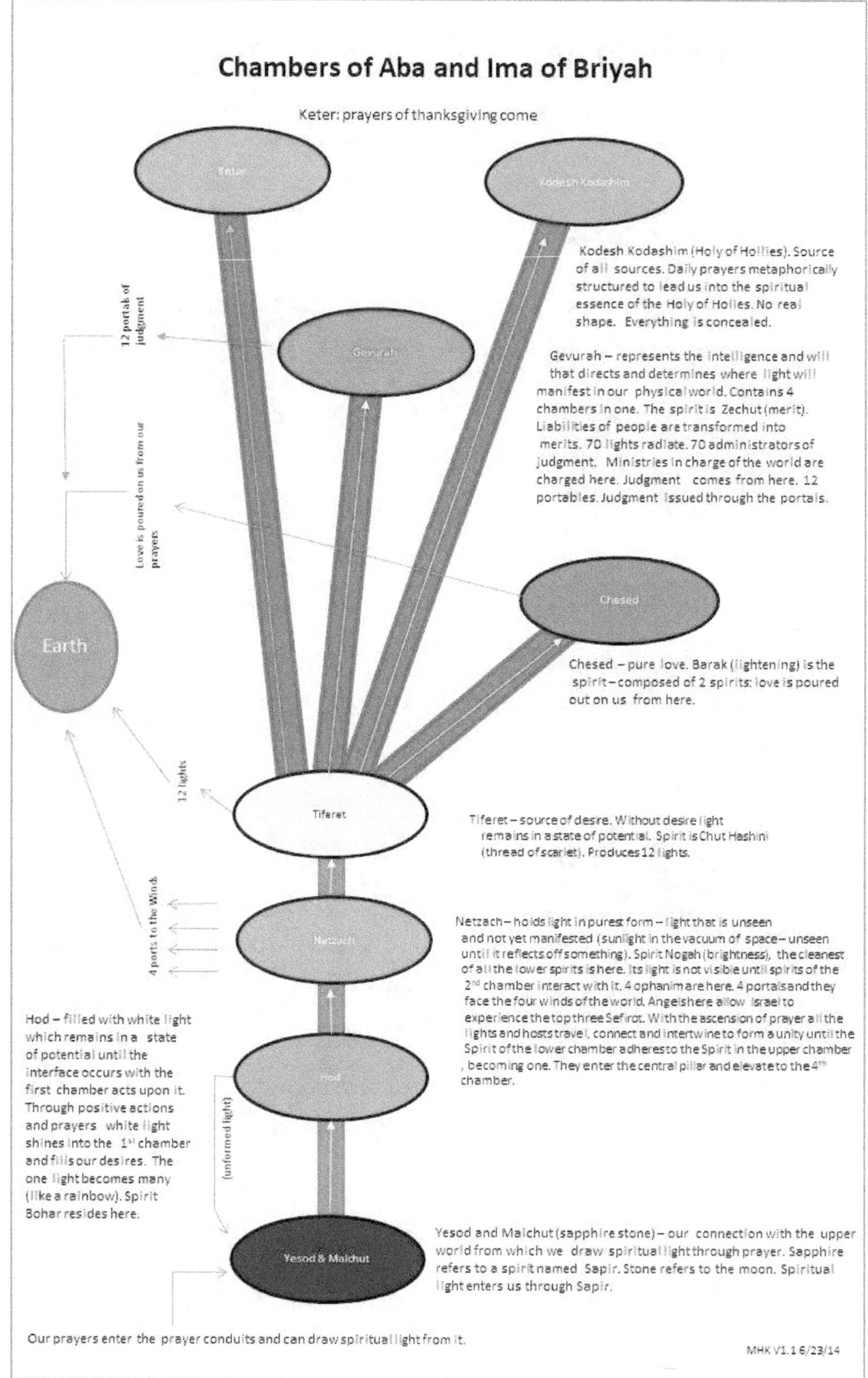
Chambers of Aba and Ima of Briyah
Keter: prayers of thanksgiving come
Keter
Kodesh Kodashim
12 portals of judgment
Gevurah
Kodesh Kodashim (Holy of Hollies). Source of all sources. Daily prayers metaphorically structured to lead us into the spiritual essence of the Holy of Hollies. No real shape. Everything is concealed.
Gevurah – represents the intelligence and will that directs and determines where light will manifest in our physical world. Contains 4 chambers in one. The spirit is Zechut (merit). Liabilities of people are transformed into merits. 70 lights radiate. 70 administrators of judgment. Ministries in charge of the world are charged here. Judgment comes from here. 12 portables. Judgment issued through the portals.
Love is poured on us from our prayers
Earth
Chesed
Chesed – pure love. Barak (lightening) is the spirit – composed of 2 spirits: love is poured out on us from here.
12 lights
Tiferet
Tiferet – source of desire. Without desire light remains in a state of potential. Spirit is Chut Hashini (thread of scarlet). Produces 12 lights.
4 ports to the Winds
Netzach
Netzach – holds light in purest form – light that is unseen and not yet manifested (sunlight in the vacuum of space – unseen until it reflects off something). Spirit Nogah (brightness), the cleanest of all the lower spirits is here. Its light is not visible until spirits of the 2nd chamber interact with it. 4 ophanim are here. 4 portals and they face the four winds of the world. Angels here allow Israel to experience the top three Sefirot. With the ascension of prayer all the lights and hosts travel, connect and intertwine to form a unity until the Spirit of the lower chamber adheres to the Spirit in the upper chamber, becoming one. They enter the central pillar and elevate to the 4th chamber.
Hod – filled with white light which remains in a state of potential until the interface occurs with the first chamber acts upon it. Through positive actions and prayers white light shines into the 1st chamber and fills our desires. The one light becomes many (like a rainbow). Spirit Bohar resides here.
Hod
(unformed light)
Yesod & Malchut
Yesod and Malchut (sapphire stone) – our connection with the upper world from which we draw spiritual light through prayer. Sapphire refers to a spirit named Sapir. Stone refers to the moon. Spiritual light enters us through Sapir.
Our prayers enter the prayer conduits and can draw spiritual light from it.
MHK V1.1 6/23/14

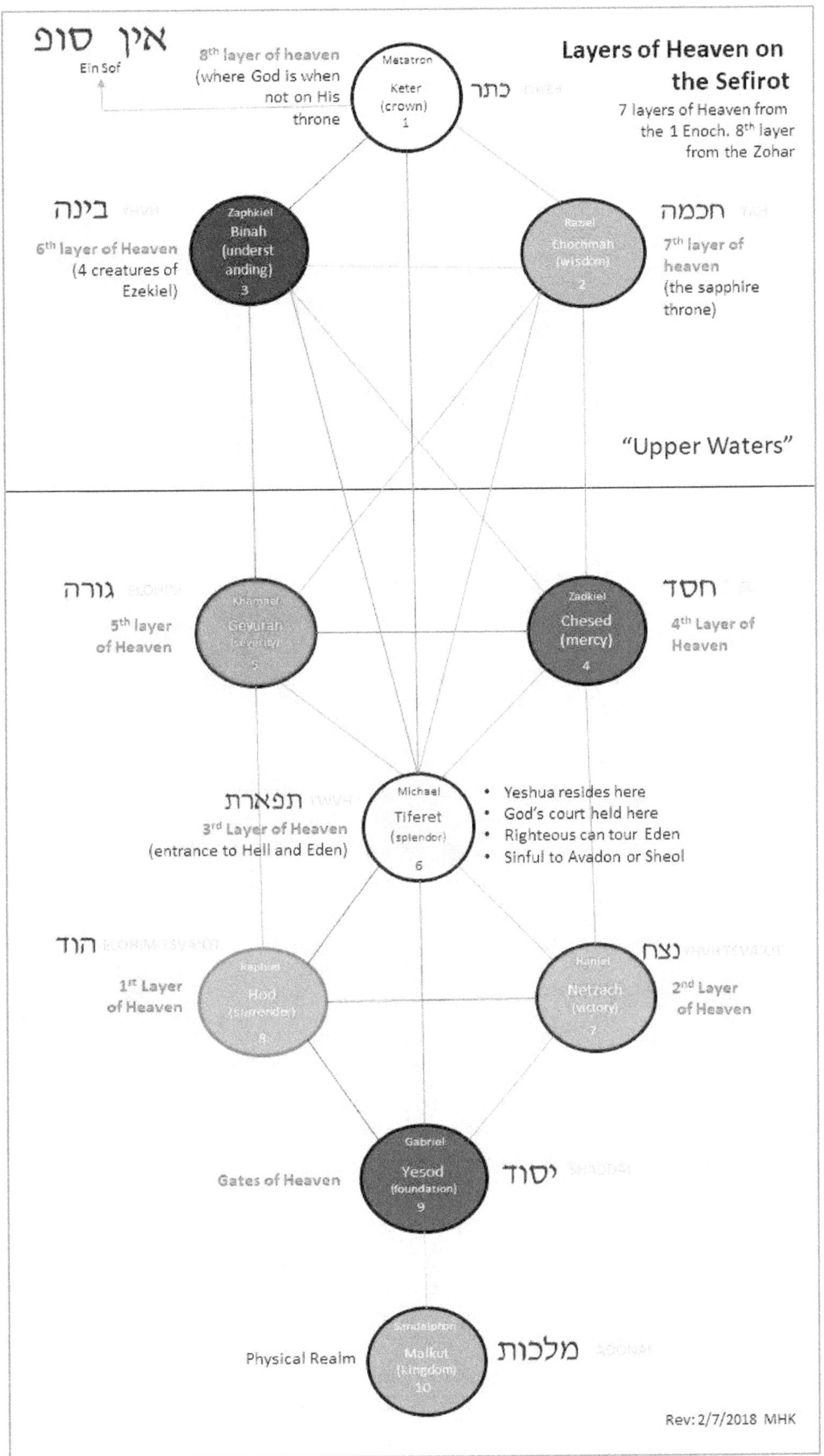
אין סוף
Ein Sof

8th layer of heaven (where God is when not on His throne)

Metatron
Keter (crown)
1

כתר

Layers of Heaven on the Sefirot
7 layers of Heaven from the 1 Enoch. 8th layer from the Zohar

בינה
6th layer of Heaven (4 creatures of Ezekiel)

Zaphkiel
Binah (understanding)
3

Raziel
Chochmah (wisdom)
2

חכמה
7th layer of heaven (the sapphire throne)

"Upper Waters"

גבורה
5th layer of Heaven

Khamael
Gevurah (severity)
5

Zadkiel
Chesed (mercy)
4

חסד
4th Layer of Heaven

תפארת
3rd Layer of Heaven (entrance to Hell and Eden)

Michael
Tiferet (splendor)
6

Yeshua resides here
God's court held here
Righteous can tour Eden
Sinful to Avadon or Sheol

הוד
1st Layer of Heaven

Raphael
Hod (surrender)
8

Haniel
Netzach (victory)
7

נצח
2nd Layer of Heaven

Gates of Heaven

Gabriel
Yesod (foundation)
9

יסוד

Physical Realm

Sandalphon
Malkut (kingdom)
10

מלכות

Rev: 2/7/2018 MHK